ANCIENT EGYPTIAN, MESOPOTAMIAN AND PERSIAN COSTUME

A TECHNICAL HISTORY
OF COSTUME

by Mary G. Houston

I

ANCIENT EGYPTIAN, MESOPOTAMIAN
AND PERSIAN COSTUME

II

ANCIENT GREEK, ROMAN AND
BYZANTINE COSTUME

III

MEDIEVAL COSTUME
IN ENGLAND AND FRANCE

PLATE I

1. ANCIENT EGYPTIAN GODDESS   2. ANCIENT EGYPTIAN QUEEN
3. ANI, A SCRIBE   4. ANCIENT EGYPTIAN QUEEN

ANCIENT EGYPTIAN
MESOPOTAMIAN
& PERSIAN COSTUME

AND DECORATION

BY

MARY G. HOUSTON

SECOND EDITION
WITH NINE PLATES, AND OVER
250 DRAWINGS IN THE TEXT

BARNES & NOBLE · NEW YORK

FIRST PUBLISHED 1920
SECOND EDITION 1954
REPRINTED 1964

MADE IN GREAT BRITAIN
PRINTED BY MORRISON AND GIBB LTD.
LONDON AND EDINBURGH

INTRODUCTION

THE costumes illustrated in this volume have been considered primarily from the technical point of view, that is, their *construction* has been carefully studied. Each type has been actually cut out draped or made up before being sketched, except of course in the case of those examples which are in the nature of duplicates. In the last of the styles, however —the Persian—where there is no elaborate draping, only one example of cutting out is given. The plates have been drawn by F. S. Hornblower.

Throughout the book the illustrations are drawn after the manner of the artists of each period, in facsimile as it were, and thus, in addition to the study of historic costume, it is possible to follow the art of representation as it develops from century to century. In addition to the contemporary drawings, however, it is necessary, for the perfect understanding of costume construction, to append a modern illustration to explain the somewhat unintelligible efforts of the archaic artist. This has been done when needful, and in each case the sketch is from an actual draping upon an artist's lay figure. Plans to scale from these lay figure draperies are also given so that the costumes can be reconstructed without difficulty.

MARY G. HOUSTON

NOTE ON THE SECOND EDITION

THE preparation of a second edition has made it possible to amplify the original work. Section II, entitled *Assyrian Costume* in the first edition, is now more aptly described as *Mesopotamian Costume*, thus embracing the Sumerian and Babylonian as well as the Assyrian styles.

In Section III, *Persian Costume*, the period described has been extended up to the time of the Islamic Conquest, as Persian Costume, though little known in the past, is of special interest owing to its being a trousered style, strongly contrasting with Sections I and II. Special thanks are due to the authorities at the British Museum and the Victoria and Albert Museum, and to the Linenhall Library, Belfast, for the facilities they have afforded me for research while preparing a second edition of this volume.

M. G. H.

CONTENTS

SECTION I

ANCIENT EGYPTIAN COSTUME

SECTION II

ANCIENT MESOPOTAMIAN COSTUME

SECTION III

ANCIENT PERSIAN COSTUME

LIST OF PLATES

ANCIENT EGYPTIAN COSTUME

INTRODUCTION

In this section Ancient Egyptian costume is described,
together with some examples of the dress of those foreign
nations whose figures are so frequently depicted in Egyptian
sculptured and painted wall-decorations. A special chapter
is devoted to Hittite costume.

When studying the costume of any country or period
we find, in the case of Ancient Egypt alone, that we are
confronted with an extraordinary conservatism or per-
sistence of style, not only through centuries but even
through milleniums.

This statement, however, must be qualified, for it is a fact that in the latest stages of Ancient Egyptian civilization as, for example, that of the long line of monarchs who reigned after the Alexandrian conquest, these Ptolemaic Pharaohs of the sculptures and paintings did not, in fact, wear the garments in which they were depicted by the Egyptian artists of the period, but rather were habited in the Greek dress of their conquering ancestors.

In addition, we have the archaistic revival of the 26th (Saite) Dynasty, 661–525 B.C., where a renaissance of the art of the Old Kingdom became the vogue, so that, in the tomb of a Saite noble of this period, at Thebes, the whole of the costumes are copied, in facsimile, from tomb pictures of the 6th Dynasty, and it is difficult for anyone not an expert to decide to which date the Saite costume really belongs. Yet in life this nobleman was certainly clad in the more elaborate dress of his own time.

The archaistic modes as represented in the tombs during this late period have been compared by Egyptologists to the seventeenth- and eighteenth-century fashion in Europe, where kings and noblemen were represented as clad in the armour or in the toga of Ancient Rome, which they certainly never wore in actual life.

This is not to say that Egyptian costume shews no changes or developments throughout its incredibly long history of over 3,000 years. Those which do appear, however, are not of a striking magnitude save in one instance, namely, at the period of that great break in Egyptian history known as the domination of the Hyksos or Shepherd Kings, who invaded and conquered Egypt, bringing from their native Asia, among other things, a distinctly new element into the dress of the Egyptians.

We are well aware of these changes in costume when a great revival in native art took place after the Hyksos had been driven out and the Egyptian Pharaohs of the great 18th Dynasty ruled the land. Yet it may be said that these changes were in the nature of additions and developments based upon the old style of dress, which never completely disappeared.

To give a comprehensive list of the dates of each of the Egyptian kings from Menes of the 1st Dynasty to Cleopatra, who was the last monarch of the 33rd Dynasty, would be beyond the scope of this volume and, for those seeking it, the information is readily accessible in the works of numerous Egyptologists.

It will be helpful at the same time to give a few of the most outstanding dates in sequence. This sequence is generally agreed upon by most authorities, though by some it is placed at an earlier epoch in the world's history than by others. It will be obvious that, for the sake of consistency, the dates here given must be chosen from the works of one of the two datings only.

The dynasties of the rulers of Egypt have been divided into those of :

"The Old Kingdom," including 1st to 8th Dynasties, 3407 B.C.

"The Middle Kingdom," including 9th to 17th Dynasties, 2111 B.C.—this Middle Kingdom covers the Hyksos period of the 15th to 17th Dynasties.

"The New Kingdom or Empire," including the 18th to 26th Dynasties, 1596 B.C.

The Persian Conquest, including 27th to 32nd Dynasties, 525 B.C.

The Greek Conquest coincides with the 33rd Dynasty, 332 B.C.–50 B.C.

The Roman Era which followed corresponded with the disappearance of Ancient Egyptian costume and ornament in its pure form.

Fig. 1.

CHAPTER I

COSTUMES OF THE OLD KINGDOM

THE very simple costumes of the Old Kingdom consisted of a kilt of varying lengths for men, and for women a tight-fitting tunic reaching from breast to ankles and kept in place by braces passing over each shoulder. Both sexes are occasionally seen wearing a cloak of thick material.

Among the most ancient representations of Egyptian costume which are known to us is that of the figure of the pre-dynastic King Narmer (3407 B.C.). In Fig. I he is seen wearing the tall white crown of Upper Egypt (the " Het "), also a plain corselet held in place by one brace, and a short plain kilt with a belt from which ornamental pendants hang down in front. Each pendant has at the top a representation of the goddess Hathor's head, and this is shewn at the side of the figure to a larger scale. At the back of the belt is fastened the ceremonial animal's tail which persists as a part of the kings of Egypt until the end of their history. On the chin of Narmer we see the ceremonial artificial beard of a king, which is fastened by straps to his crown. The figure of this king is taken from that very ancient fragment decorated with figures in relief and called " The Palette of Narmer," a memorial tablet shewing the king in battle. The beards of gods, kings and noblemen were each different in shape, each symbolic of their wearers. This symbolism, so intricate in its character and so pre-

5

dominantly a feature of the dress of the Egyptian gods, is often transferred to the royal costumes ; hence we see a king in the dress of a god, and frequently both gods and goddesses are represented as wearing the crowns of Upper and Lower Egypt (*see* Plate I).

In the present volume the costumes are considered mainly as being examples of period and silhouette, and also from the constructive or technical viewpoint ; but in the bibliography appended on pp. 188 there are given the names of books dealing specially with Ancient Egyptian symbolism, and perhaps one of the most informative in connection with this aspect of costume is *The Gods of the Egyptians*, by Sir E. A. Wallis Budge (1904), which has numerous plates in colour of the gods in their symbolic costumes. In *Manners and Customs of the Ancient Egyptians* by Sir J. Gardner Wilkinson (ed. 1878) there is also special information on symbolic costume.

Figs. 2 and 3.—The Princess Sedet and Prince Nereb are shewn to be wearing the typical dress of persons of distinction at the period of the Old Kingdom, 4th Dynasty (2789 B.C.– 2715 B.C.). The figures are after Lepsius, who describes them as being from the Pyramid of Giseh. The tunic of the woman is red, her collar blue and white, her wig black and skin beige colour. The kilt of the man is white with the pleated part in gold, his wig is black and his skin is coloured reddish-brown. The early appearance of the characteristic orna-mental-beaded collar in both figures is noteworthy, also the fact that wigs are worn even at this early period. The heads of the men were shaven or cut very close, probably for the sake of cleanliness and save in the case of persons of the lower social classes and the priesthood, wigs were worn. Among women, however, the custom of shaving the head

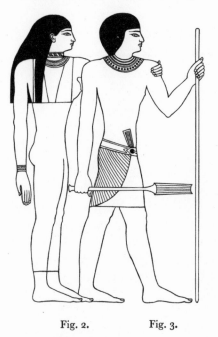

Fig. 2.   Fig. 3.

was not universal. The hair was either allowed to grow or
cut short, rather than shaved, though covered with a wig.
At one period, indeed, during the 18th Dynasty, a fashion
of shaving the heads of ladies does appear to have been the
vogue for a short time. The well-known bust of Queen
Nerfertiti and several other portraits shew shaven heads
without wigs. The wigs of ladies of high rank were more
elaborate and bulky than those of men, but with women
mourners at funerals the natural hair, worn hanging simply
down the back, was the rule.

Figs. 4 and 5 of the same period as Figs. 2 and 3 (also
from Lepsius, Giseh) shew two other examples of the kilt,
while Fig. 3 gives us one of the earliest pleated or gauffered
types. Figs. 4 and 5 introduce us to the very ancient practice

of stiffening these linen garments and with an evident striving after effect and silhouette which seems extraordinarily sophisticated at such a very remote era.

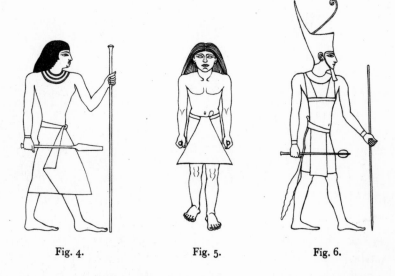

Fig. 4.   Fig. 5.   Fig. 6.

Fig. 6 is an example of the costume of the early kings of Egypt which was retained in later ages as the costume of the gods. It is after Lepsius, who entitles it " from a tomb of the 5th Dynasty at Wadi Maghara." Here we have the red crown (the " Teser ") of Lower or Northern Egypt, a corselet held up by braces, a kilt with ornamental pendant in front and animal's tail at the back. The whole drawing is without detail, but one need only compare it with later examples to realize that the chief features of this costume remain identical in silhouette for more than three milleniums.

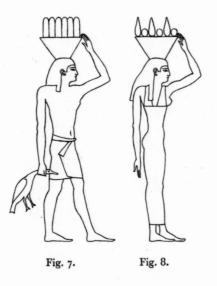

Fig. 7.   Fig. 8.

COSTUME OF THE WORKERS

Figs. 7 and 8 (after Lepsius and from Giseh) shew a man and woman of the 4th Dynasty, carrying provisions. When comparing them with Figs. 2 and 3 we see that here the handsome-beaded collars of the princess and her husband are absent, and that the man's kilt is without ornament. Apart from the detail, however, the costumes are very similar. Figs. 9, 10 and 11, also after Lepsius, who describes Fig. 9 as being of the 6th Dynasty and from Sarriet-el-Meilin, as is also Fig. 10, while Fig. 11, that of a scribe taking notes on a tablet and with a pen behind his ear, Lepsius quotes as of the 5th Dynasty and from Giseh.

2

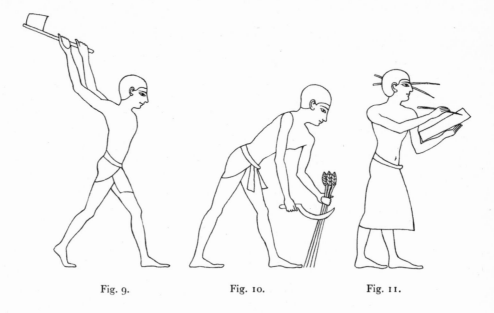

Fig. 9.   Fig. 10.   Fig. 11.

HEAD-DRESSES OF THE OLD KINGDOM

These head-dresses are comparatively simple in style when compared with those of the later dynasties. Typical examples are Figs. 12, 13 and 14, taken from early sculptures. Fig. 13 of the 4th Dynasty is from the statue of the Princess Nefert. The original statue is in the Cairo Museum where the princess is seen seated beside her husband, Prince Rahetep. Her natural hair shews on her forehead under her wig. The circlet on her head is decorated with rosettes alternating with flowers in profile. She has a cloak over her tunic, which garment, as has been said, was worn occasionally by both sexes at this period. This garment appears to have been of thick material, but it is represented in a manner so

Fig. 12.   Fig. 14.

Fig. 17.   Fig. 13   Fig. 18.

conventional that it is difficult to conjecture its construction
or cut. We may, however, consider, that in harmony with
the other garments worn at this time, it was of simple
rectangular shape. In length these cloaks reached to the
ankles. Figs. 12 and 14 are " Ti," a celebrated architect,
and " Ranefer," a high priest, both of the 5th Dynasty and
both from the original statues in the Cairo Museum. These
two heads shew examples of the types of wig worn by men
in the period of the Old Kingdom.

JEWELLERY

The jewellery of this era is not so profuse as is that of
the Middle Kingdom and New Empire, but mention may be
made of four very beautiful bracelets found in the grave of

the queen of " King Ler " of the 1st Dynasty and illustrated, in colour, in the *Journal of Egyptian Exploration*. Three of these bracelets are of beads, varied and exquisite in design and consisting of gold, turquoise and amethyst beads alternating. The fourth bracelet is perhaps the most attractive of all. It consists of twenty-seven little plaques of turquoise and pure gold alternating. At the top of each plaque there is a tiny " hawk of Horus " perched upon a square plinth which simulates the doorway of a house and symbolizes the " Eternal Abode." Here, as in the bead bracelets, there is an originality and sense of proportion in the design which, in spite of great simplicity, has seldom been surpassed by the jewellery of any age.

To conclude : the costumes of the Old Kingdom are the foundation of Egyptian dress until the Roman Era, and again all the changes which take place during the Middle Kingdom and the New Empire are in the nature of additions —the old survive alongside the new.

CHAPTER II

THE MIDDLE KINGDOM

THOUGH there is little change in the types of costume worn
by the men and women of the period of the Middle Kingdom
when compared with that of the former age, in it the arts
of Egypt reached what is said by experts to be their apogee
of delicacy and taste during the Central Period, namely, that
of the 12th Dynasty (2111 B.C.–1898 B.C.). The jewellery
was specially fine. Fig. 15 is perhaps the most beautiful
example, and is a royal diadem which was found at Illahoun.
This diadem was part of the jewellery of the " Princess Sat-
hathor-ant," wife of Amenemhat III. It consists of a flat
circlet of gold rather more than an inch wide, and encrusted
with fifteen small golden rosettes with cloisonné inlays and
jewels. In front, set into a little slot, there is a golden
uraeus, beautifully modelled in the round, with eyes of
garnet set in a lapis-lazuli head, its body inlaid with cloisonné
of carnelian and lapis. At the back of the circlet rise two
tall golden feathers of gold plate, so thin that they must
have quivered and flashed with every movement of the
wearer. At the back and also at either side hang down thin
golden streamers, in pairs, which are attached to the circlet
by loose rings so as to give with each turn of the head. The
original of this diadem is in the Cairo Museum, but there is a
wonderful reproduction of it in the Metropolitan Museum of
New York, and this has been set upon a reconstructed wig of

the period, which has thin plaits of hair hanging down all round, each ending in a tiny curl. At close intervals all round the wig hang down strings of tubular gold beads of the same length as the plaits and each string of beads enclosing a strand of hair which ends, like the plaits, in a little curl.

Fig. 15.

Fig. 16.

Fig. 16 is a detail from another 12th Dynasty treasure in the Cairo Museum which is known as " the diadem of the Princess Khnumit," which was found at Daschow. This is a circlet in pierced gold work and is composed of front and side views of conventionalized flowers alternating, from which rise vertically other flowers in profile. The whole is set with precious stones, and in the centre front two of the repeats are bridged over by a hovering falcon. This circlet is not a royal crown, but merely a diadem for personal adornment.

For comparison of such diadems in wear with the actual examples at Figs. 15 and 16, *see* Figs. 17 and 18, after Prisse d'Avennes, who describes Fig. 17 as of the 6th Dynasty and Fig. 18 of the 12th Dynasty. Another interesting comparison is that of the design of this circlet, Fig. 16, with the design of the simple example shewn in wear at Fig. 13. There can be little doubt that the design of the later circlet is founded on the same model as Fig. 13.

Besides that deep jewelled or beaded collar, which was the most characteristic, ornamental feature of all in Egyptian costume, the pendant or pectoral hanging over the breast from a chain round the neck and kept in position by a counter-

Fig. 19.

weight at the back is of most frequent occurrence.   Fig 19
is a 12th Dynasty pectoral, found at Illahoun.   It is part of
the jewellery of the " Princess Sit-hathor-ant."   In the middle
of the top of this ornament is the cartouche or nameplate of
Senusert II and on either side a uraeus, the tail of which
passes through the ring of an " ankh " and then encompasses
a circle of carnelian.   Below is a kneeling figure, holding
palm branches, from whose right arm is suspended a tadpole.
On either side again, are two hawks, each with a claw pressed
against the palm branches.   The whole is in pierced gold

work with inlays of carnelian and lapis lazuli. The eyes of the hawks are of garnet. The reverse side of the pectoral is of plain gold, but beautifully engraved and chased. The chain of beads which suspend the pectoral are of drop-shaped carnelian, felspar and lapis lazuli alternating and separated by small spherical beads of gold and turquoise alternating. The whole design is a motto which reads " The Sun-God gives many hundreds and thousands of years to Senusert II."

This type of pectoral occurs frequently as an ornament subsequent to the 12th Dynasty, but the execution and design of the later jewellery did not reach such a high standard.

Figs. 20 and 21 are after Lepsius, who describes them as of the 12th Dynasty from the rock-tombs at Berscheh. They are examples of unusual costumes, and of interest as shewing a short cape and enveloping shawl of thick striped

Fig. 20.   Fig. 21.   Fig. 24

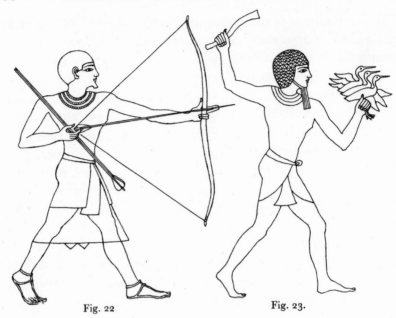

Fig. 22   Fig. 23.

material in wear, also in Fig. 20 a long robe of transparent
linen worn over a short kilt of thicker stuff. Fig. 22 again
shews two similar kilts in wear and Fig. 23 shews a short kilt
with small apron pendant. Both Figs. 22 and 23 are after
Lepsius, who assigns them to the 12th Dynasty and from a
tomb at Beni Hassan.

Fig. 24 is after Prisse d'Avennes who describes the costume
as being that of a native of Punt (Somaliland) and of the
17th Dynasty. The man here depicted is in the act of
driving a laden ass. This figure would belong to the period
between the Hyksos kings and the revival under the 18th
Dynasty. The tailpiece to this chapter, Fig. 25, is after
Lepsius, who describes it as of the 12th Dynasty and from
Beni Hassan. The figures of the women dancers are in two
groups—each a miming ballet—that on the left representing

the Pharaoh about to slay his captive, whom, in typical attitude, he holds by the hair. The three figures on the right are supposed to represent " the wind." The hair of each of the dancers is tied up in the shape of a certain type of royal crown and they wear the short kilts of men.

Fig. 25.

CHAPTER III

COSTUME IN THE NEW EMPIRE, COMMENCING
WITH THOSE OF THE 18TH DYNASTY (1576 B.C.)

AT this period we are conscious of a greater elaboration in
Egyptian costume. Asiatic influences coming into the
country with the Hyksos had introduced or at least made
popular two very voluminous new garments, which may be
described as the *Robe* and the *Shawl.* The Robe, which is
still in wear in present-day Egypt, is identical in cut with the
" Royal Robe of Persia," but it must have been introduced
into Eastern Asia and from thence to Egypt at a date far
anterior to the Persian conquests. The long narrow Shawl,
which was draped round the body in various ways, was worn
chiefly by women and seems to have come from India, or at
least from " the Land of Elam " on the eastern side of the
Persian Gulf, for we find it there as early as 2000 B.C.
(Figs. 96, 97, 98, p.93, Elamite Lady). There was nothing
of the primitive in the Egyptian weaving of the New
Empire. Petrie tells us that the looms could, on occasion,
manufacture a cloth of five feet in width, and the finest
linens were wellnigh transparent. The almost universal
fashion of gauffering or pleating, which from this time onwards seems to have been applied to the fine linen costumes
now worn, gives them their most distinctive note, though
this pleating was used to some small extent from the earliest
ages. Besides these new and important-looking garments

the wigs and head-dresses of this period began to exhibit the greatest elaboration and variety, so that a considerable volume might be filled with the details of the costume alone.

Another innovation of the period was that of armour in the form of coats or hauberks of mail, which was chiefly an Asiatic introduction.

In addition to the costume of the native Egyptians of the New Empire we have most interesting and accurate representations of the dress of foreigners who were either of tributary nations or captives taken in battle by the Egyptians. Some again are representations of mercenary soldiers, fighting for the Pharaohs and among these are the helmeted " Shordana," others are enemies such as were the pig-tailed Hittites.

In the 18th Dynasty, besides those new garments introduced from Asia and the consequent elaboration of dress, there is a certain patriotic renaissance of the simpler 12th Dynasty style in the arts generally, including that of costume, which is characteristic of the beginning of this era. The 12th Dynasty influences soon disappeared, however, and in the dynasties immediately following the 18th, increasing elaboration was the rule. The examples given to illustrate this period and others throughout this volume have not been chosen because of any historic interest in the person of the wearers of the costumes, but rather have been selected to illustrate the introduction of new and varied styles of dress. It would indeed be a lengthy task to give a costume portrait of the immensely long list of Egyptian monarchs and their consorts, and one which would lead to wearisome repetitions of almost identical costumes in many cases.

Again the types selected to illustrate the costumes and

head-dresses of the gods have been confined to a very few of the most striking and important examples, as Sir E. A. Wallis Budge in his book *The Gods of Egypt*, to which reference has already been made, has treated this subject with the greatest completeness, and it will be gathered from this authority that the matter is more of the nature of a study in symbolism than of varied styles of costume.

Fig. 26 is given at full length to shew the typical costume of a god among the ancient Egyptians. Here we see the collar, corselet and kilt which may be said to be almost uniformly worn except in cases where there is a completely different dress indicating another aspect of the god's person (*see* Osiris, Plate II). On the other hand, the head-dresses of these sacred personages shew much variety, and it is here that the special symbolic element is so important. The head-dress of Fig. 26 is that of the god " Amen-Ra," who is also represented in four other forms (*see* Budge). At Fig. 26 he is shewn as a man, holding in one hand the sceptre (" nas ") and in the other the war-knife (" klepesh "). He wears a flat-topped cap, out of which spring two tall feathers, a pendant from the cap falls almost to the ground. He has the usual wide-jewelled or beaded collar ; his corselet, held up by braces, is covered with a scale pattern, which Petrie tells us probably indicates that it is made of feathers. His kilt and belt date from the time of the Old Kingdom. The drawing is after Champollion, who describes it as being from Ilsamboul in Nubia, and states that the god is presenting the war-knife to Rameses III.

The colouring of Fig. 26 is as follows : feathers, red and green ; cap, red ; all the flesh is coloured blue ; corselet, gold with pattern in red and **green** ; kilt, gold.

The typical head-dress of Osiris is that of the white crown of Upper Egypt with a curling plume at either side, is given at Plate II.   Some authorities refer to this as the "Atef" Crown (*see* B.M. Catalogue). Besides these two comparatively simple head-dresses pertaining to Amen-Ra and Osiris there is the "Atef" Crown as described by Wallis Budge who defines it as "a crown consisting of plumes, disk and horns."   This head-dress is worn by the crocodile god Sebek-Ra, but, as has already been said, in the later periods of Egyptian art such head-dresses are worn by kings and gods alike.

Fig. 27 is a somewhat elaborate development of this crown (the Atef Crown, according to Wallis Budge). The drawing is after Rossellini, who describes it as being from a wall-decoration representing the conquests

Fig. 26.

of Rameses II, Temple of Beit-nalli, Nubia.   At Fig. 27 in addition to the plumes, disk and horns, two uraei support the plumes on either side and two more hang from each horn.

Fig. 28, besides the goat's horns, disks, feathers and uraei, has a reeded ornament (" khaker-ornament ") between the feathers.   This represents the head of a papyrus reed with the fronds tied together and rising from a disk, also besides the goat's horns we see here in addition the cow's horns and disk (as worn by the goddesses Isis and Hathor).   There are also four uraei on the head-dress and another one on the forehead.   Over the ear is a ram's horn.   Here we see also the striped linen head-dress called the " Khat " (Carter) which, after being folded over the head, has the ends confined in a kind of queue which hangs down the back.   This drawing (Fig. 28) is after Lepsius, who describes it as being of the 19th Dynasty and from a tomb at Qurna.   The " Khat " as a royal head-dress is seen in the sculptures of the Old Kingdom, and in those of the New Empire it is still in being. The effigy of Tut-ankh-amen, for example, upon his golden coffin, shews the Khat, as does also a statue of the same monarch in the Cairo Museum (*see* Fig. 29).   This head-dress, as will be seen, is of a very simple type.   In complete contrast with Fig. 29 is Fig. 30, which is one of the most elaborate of all Egyptian head-dresses.   This type had a considerable vogue among the monarchs of the latest Egyptian dynasties, as, for example, during the period of the Persian Conquest (525 B.C.—27th to 32nd Dynasties).   In this connection the following note from *Perse Ancienne* by Flandin and Coste is of interest.   Here the authors mention that on the authority of Perrot, there is, in the ruins of an ancient Persian town, a bas-relief of Cyrus, clad in Assyrian costume, but wearing an Egyptian wig and head-dress, which latter he thus describes :

" Above the head two huge goat's horns branch out on either side and support an exceedingly complicated head-dress, made up of three solar disks from which emerge bundles of reed held together with a string and between them ostrich feathers.   A pair of snakes encircles the group.   The Persian artist was here influenced by

Fig. 27.

Fig. 28.

Fig. 30.

Fig. 32.

3

Fig. 29.

both Assyrian and Egyptian art—the dress Assyrian
and the head-dress Egyptian. The effort to produce,
with minute precision, one of the quaint hieratic head-
dresses of the Delta is very evident. The one chosen was
the diadem Egyptologists call the ' Hoetas,' which
appears to be the exclusive attribute of that in the older
monuments, but from the 20th Dynasty onwards forms
the head-dress of kings and gods alike."

It will be seen that this description by Perrot might well be
applied to the drawing of the head-dress at Fig. 30, which is
after Rosellini who describes it as being from the rock temple
at Kalabschieh and of the Roman Era. Besides the term
" Hoetas," quoted by Perrot, this crown is also called " the
Triple-Atef" crown by modern Egyptologists. The head at
Fig. 30 is that of the youthful god Harsiesi, whose youth is
indicated by the lock of hair, the so-called " Horus lock,"

which is seen to fall over his left ear. When shaving a young boy's head the Egyptians left a lock of hair to fall over one ear, and this became eventually the typical badge of youth, more especially it was that of the youthful god Horus and

Fig. 31.

thus called by his name. It was worn by Egyptian princes—the sons of the Pharaoh—to emphasize the fact of their subordinate position in relation towards their father—just as a royal Spanish prince was called, during his father's life-time, " the Infant."

Fig. 31 is that of a royal prince. It is after Champollion,

who describes it as being from the palace of Rameses IV at Medinet-Habu. Here the " Horus lock " is conventionalized, or perhaps encased with a portion of the head-dress designed to fit it. Rameses IV reigned during the 20th Dynasty, so that the costume here illustrated is of a late type and the era is said to be one of decadence in its art. This prince (Fig. 31) wears a corselet which seems to be embroidered. His transparent kilt and floating girdle-ends are seen in wear, however, as early as the 18th Dynasty, for the Figure of Tut-ankh-amen (1354 B.C.–1345 B.C.) is represented as clothed in a similar kilt, also the floating girdle is worn by him and by the youthful queen Ankh-es-en-Amen, where they are represented together on the back panel of the *King's Golden Throne* (vol. ii, Tut-ankh-amen, H. Carter). The renowned " Diadem of Tut-ankh-amen " is also illustrated in the above volume, and this characteristic royal ornament is of gold, inlaid with circlets of cornelian. The conventional bow at the back is also of gold and inlaid with malachite and sardonyx. The insignia in front—the hawk's head and uraeus—are exquisitely modelled in the round.

Fig. 32 shews a diadem almost identical in form with that of Tut-ankh-amen. This is after Lepsius, who describes it as from Thebes, Abd-el-Qurnah and of the 18th Dynasty. This diadem, however, shews only the uraeus over the brow, the hawk is absent.

Another royal head-dress of the New Empire is shewn at Fig. 33, also after Lepsius. This is from El Amarna and is a portrait of Amenhotep IV, better known as Akhenaton " the heretic king " (1384 B.C.–1370 B.C.), whose reign preceded that of his son-in-law, Tut-ankh-amen. The naturalistic art of the reign of Akhenaton, shewing clearly as it does the deformities of the king's face and figure, is an extraordinarily arresting feature, set amid the age-long conventionalities of Egyptian figure-drawing.

The type of head-dress seen at Fig. 33 is really a royal war-helmet (the "chepereoh"), a form which does not appear in the earlier Egyptian representations of the Pharaohs. For

Fig. 33.

the rest, Akhenaton wears a simple type of pleated kilt (the "shendy-kilt") with small pendant apron in front, ceremonial tail at the back and his feet are in sandals. Two ribbons hang down from the back of his helmet, exactly in the manner of those ribbons or "infulae" which are attached to the mitre of a bishop of the Catholic Church.

Fig. 34.

Fig. 34 shews the whole costume, with details of head-dress, deep collar, belt and apron, of Rameses III (20th Dynasty, 1207 B.C.–1101 B.C.). The drawing is after Champollion, who describes it as being from the Necropolis at Thebes. Here we have an excellent representation of the new Robe which came into fashion with the 18th Dynasty. (The method of cutting out and draping this garment is explained in detail in Chapter VII).

In Fig. 34 the robe of Rameses is the usual white, semi-transparent, pleated linen. The " Khat " head-dress is here, not of the ordinarily simple type such as is seen at Fig. 29, but over and above the usual simple striping, it is decorated with a hawk at the back and six extra uraei at either side, two of them crowned and placed at either side of the forehead, and a row of four with disks at the bottom of the side pendants. In addition a larger uraeus projects over the centre of the forehead and the side view of a crown surmounting the " Khat " shews seven of these symbols surrounding it, each again crowned with a disk. The deep collar or yoke also shews two hawks, and there is hanging from the belt an elaborate apron-pendant. It is of interest to note that an actual specimen of one of these decorative pendants was found in the tomb of Tut-ankh-amen, which is made up of golden plaques inlaid with polychrome glass, these plaques are threaded together by means of small beads. We may infer that the central strip of the apron at Fig. 34 would be of similar make-up. The strips at either side of the central pendant give the impression of having been made of painted or encrusted leather. The belt, like one which was found in the tomb of Tut-ankh-amen, was probably of chased gold and inlaid with coloured glass. The king's " cartouche " or name-plate is seen in the centre of the pendant. The cartouche also forms the clasp of the belt and it is repeated again on the bracelets. As the head-dresses of the gods were worn by the kings, so also among the Egyptian queens we find that the head-dresses of the most popular goddesses were frequently adopted.   The well-known hawk head-dress of Isis (*see* Plate I) with the cow's horns and moon's disk of Hathor are seen repeatedly in the head-dresses of the queens of the New Empire.

Figs. 35 and 36 are given at full length to shew the usual costume of Egyptian goddesses ; they are after Gardner-Wilkinson. Fig. 35 is the goddess Anka, Anonkis or Anuket. " Her feather head-dress seems to point to a foreign origin

Fig. 35.   Fig. 36.

but her worship appears as early as the 12th Dynasty " (Wilkinson). She has in her right hand the " ankh " or symbol of life, and in her left she carries the characteristic " flower sceptre " of a goddess.

Fig. 36 is the goddess of truth—Ma or Maat.   The single feather is her distinctive emblem.

Fig. 37 is from the statue of Queen Amenerites in the Cairo Museum.   Here we have a comparatively simple type of head-dress, which is worn also by Queen Aahmes Nefertari, wife of Aahmes, who reigned early in the 18th Dynasty.   It

Fig. 37.

consists of the hawk head-dress of Isis with a uraeus on either side of the head of the hawk and a lofty crown encircled by uraei surmounting it.   The whole is placed upon a huge padded wig.   The drawing is after Prisse d'Avennes.

A more elaborate example is shewn at Fig. 38.   This is a portrait of Queen Taia or Tiy, queen of Amenophis III. Here, above the Isis hawk head-dress and the crown as shewn at Fig. 37, we have again a hawk wearing the white crown and supporting plumes of Osiris, while in front of it there are two asps or uraei with disks on their heads.   This

Fig. 38.

queen is wearing the shawl or " sari " type of dress, characteristic of women's court costumes in the days of the New Empire. The drawing is after Prisse d'Avennes.

Fig. 39 is from a sculptured stele in the British Museum (No. 811) and is a portrait of Queen Ankhnes Neferatra,

Fig. 39.   Fig. 40.

queen of Amasis II (26th Dynasty). This shews the hawk head-dress of Isis, the horns and disk of Hathor and the two feathers called " suti." This figure is draped in the shawl or sari, and the arrangement here is very similar to that shewn on a lay figure at Fig. 97. The queen carries the sceptre or crook and the flail, its complement, both of which are the insignia of Osiris.

At Fig. 31 was given the portrait of a royal prince wearing the Horus-lock head-dress. Fig. 40 is the portrait of a princess from the same source, namely, the palace of Rameses IV, Medinet Habu. The princess has a short wig or cap, and at one side a very conventional Horus lock held in place by a circlet. This is surmounted by an ornament consisting of two feathers and a papyrus flower. She is dressed in the full robe of the New Empire and carries in her right hand the sacred " systrum " (a species of rattle). The final illustration of the Horus lock in its most attractive form is from a portrait of Rameses II (19th Dynasty) at Fig. 41. He wears the circlet diadem, with uraeus entwined and a short wig from which the Horus lock depends. Three streamers hang down from the base of his wig at the back and he wears a leopard skin over his wide jewelled collar. The drawing is after Prisse d'Avennes.

Fig. 42 is drawn from the well-known bust of Queen Nefertiti. The original of this bust is in the Berlin Museum, to which reference has been made in Chapter I, as shewing that at this period during the 18th Dynasty the masculine fashion of shaving the head seems to have been extended to women, at least to those of royal rank. Not the slightest vestige of hair is seen in this portrait nor in drawings of the queen wearing the same head-dress, where she is represented in the company of her husband, Ankhenaton ; her young daughters wearing no head-dress also seem to have closely shaven heads. This head-dress at Fig. 42 resembles in some

Fig. 41.

Fig. 42.   Fig. 43.

degree the high cap worn by the god Amen-ra (*see* Fig. 26).
Round the cap of Nefertiti a fillet similar to the diadem of
Tut-ankh-amen, is tied.   The uraeus in front of the cap is
slightly defaced in the original, but has been restored in the
drawing at Fig. 42.

Fig. 43 is after Champollion, who describes the subject as
" the divine nurse " (or governess) of Amenophis II in his
youth, and as being from the Acropolis at Thebes (18th
Dynasty).   It will be seen to have a close resemblance to
Fig. 18, p. 11 in the type of wig worn and in the character
of the decorative fillet or head-band.   Fig. 43 is, however,
full of interesting detail which is absent in the 12th Dynasty
example.

The drawing at Fig. 44 is after Champollion, who describes it as " scene from the toilet of a lady, Thebes, Kourna ; tomb painting from the grand palace of Mene-pha I " (19th Dynasty).

Fig. 44.

Fig. 45.

CHAPTER IV

MILITARY COSTUME, CHIEFLY THAT OF THE NEW EMPIRE

BEFORE illustrating the dress of the ordinary Egyptian soldier, Figs. 45, 46 and 47 are examples of the Pharaoh, Rameses III, in different types of military costume. The drawings are after Champollion and Prisse d'Avennes. In Fig. 45, which is described by Champollion as being from Abu Simbel in Nubia, we see the king with bow, quiver and war axe. He wears the " double crown " (" pshert ") of Upper and Lower Egypt, a ceremonial beard, and under his broad beaded collar he has that type of " cross over " corselet which is illustrated upon a lay figure and its cut explained at Fig. 101, *a* and *b*, Chapter VII. His belt, kilt and tail are all traditional garments dating as far back as the Old Kingdom. The arm-guard on his right arm is the archer's characteristic protection against graze or injury while shooting with the bow.

Fig. 46 is a second portrait of this Pharaoh (after Champollion and also from Abu Simbel). Here he is represented in his triumphal chariot after a victory. The officer who precedes his chariot carries the king's sandals on his arm (*see* Fig. 48). Rameses here wears the royal war-helmet (" chepresh ") with its streamers. He is not in fighting dress but wears the voluminous robe of the period, which, however, is tightly draped up under the arms in order not to impede

Fig. 46.

him as he drives his two-horsed chariot. His left hand holds his bow, while in his right he has his war-falchion and an arrow. Both hands are also engaged with the horses' reins.

In the original drawing the figure of the king is concealed by the chariot from the hips to the feet. At Fig. 46 the legs and feet have been supplied from another portrait of the king in similar costume. It should be noted here that while actually driving the chariot the king's feet were not sandalled, as the floor of that vehicle being most probably made of plaited reeds, he would stand on this much more firmly with naked feet. Hence the carrying of the sandals by the officer preceding him. Fig. 47 is after Prisse d'Avennes, who

Fig. 47.

describes the drawing as illustrating " the combat of Rameses III against the Khétas on the banks of the Orontes," and gives the source of the work as the Ramasseum at Thebes. The king wears, in this picture, a close-fitting coat of mail which is of Asiatic origin and seems identical in style with the hauberks of the Assyrians. It was most probably made of leather or linen sewn over with plates of metal or bone. The lower part of the king's figure is concealed by his chariot, but the hauberk most probably reached to half-way between knee and ankle. There is nothing Asiatic, on the other hand, about the king's helmet, which is characteristically Egyptian. His pectoral, worn over a deep-beaded collar, is of similar type to the 12th Dynasty example illustrated at Fig. 19, p. 16. Rameses being engaged in combat, his horses' reins are tied round his waist in order to leave his hands free. Lack of space prevents the king's war-chariot and richly caparisoned horses from being illustrated here, but these trappings are portrayed with infinite care and skill by the Egyptian artist. In the great folios of Champollion and Prisse d'Avennes, the royal chariots are beautifully illustrated with all their elaborate ornamental details and in the original colourings. Fig. 49 shews the head of the near horse.

Fig. 48 is an officer of high rank who precedes the royal chariot in this triumphal procession. He carries a bow in his left hand and a species of staff in his right. His helmet with its fringed edge is probably made of leather and padded inside. His corselet and braces seem to be of quilted and padded linen. As has been said, he carries the royal sandals strung upon his arm, no doubt a task of honour, and this method of carrying is characteristically Egyptian.

Fig. 50 (after Champollion) shews an Egyptian warrior and his driver in a war-chariot of the period of the New

Fig. 48.

Fig. 49.

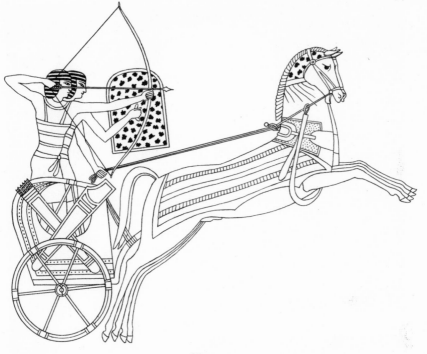

Fig. 50.

Empire. The quiverful of arrows and the empty bow-case are crossed diagonally at the side of the chariot. The driver holds a small shield to protect the fighting man, and this appears to be covered with the dappled skin of some wild animal. This chariot, though plain and simple in type, is, in its main characteristics, similar to the richly decorated one of the Pharaoh.

The chief offensive weapons of the rank and file of the Egyptian Army were the bow, spear, javelin, sword, curved falchion and battle-axe. Their defensive armour was light in character. Besides the padded helmet, they are only occasionally represented with a short cuirass or corselet of the ancient Egyptian type, reaching from breast to waist, and more seldom still they may be seen wearing a hauberk of linen covered with small plates of metal or bone, but this last defence was not in use before the days of the New Empire. Most frequently, however, the Egyptian soldier was clad merely in the usual linen kilt to which was added the helmet and a shield. This latter in early times was of very large dimensions, as can be seen at Fig. 51. This drawing is after Gardner Wilkinson, who describes it as being of the Middle

Fig. 51.

Empire and from a tomb at Siut. This soldier would be seen to be clad in a short kilt were his figure not partly hidden by his immense shield.

Fig. 52*a* and *b* are after Champollion, who describes them as a war-helmet and coat of mail from a wall-painting in the tomb of Rameses IV (19th Dynasty) and from Thebes.

Fig. 53 *a* and *b* are a sword and falchion from the same source. Figs. 54*a* (after Lepsius) and 54*b* (after Champollion) shew (*a*) an Egyptian spearman in light armour and (*b*) an archer in the hauberk and helmet. They are characteristic of the 18th and 19th Dynasties respectively. The curious

Fig. 52a.

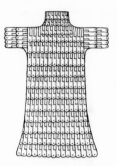

Fig. 52b.

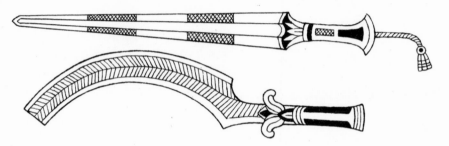

Figs. 53a and 53b.

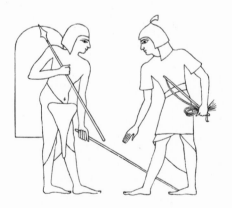

Fig. 54a.   Fig. 54b.

stiffened triangular apron which is seen in front of the spearman's kilt is a very frequent feature in the kilts of the
Egyptian soldiers during the New Empire.

Fig. 55 is after Rosellini (who describes the drawing as
being from Ibsamboul; period Rameses III) and is an
illustration of one of the mercenary soldiers who were
employed by the Egyptian Pharaohs to supplement the
native army. The men who wear this costume were called
" Shairetana " or " Shardana " by the Egyptians. While
some authorities believe these men to have been Sardinians,
others have given them an Asiatic origin. Fig. 56 is after
Champollion, who writes of it that it is from the palace of
Rameses IV, at Medinet Habu. Here we see two Philistines
in combat with an Egyptian. The Philistines are distinguished
by their characteristic feather head-dresses, they carry round
shields in contrast to the arch-shaped one of the Egyptian,

Fig. 55.

Fig. 56.

also their kilts are different and shew great similarity in shape to the kilts of the Cretans (*see* Chapter VI, Fig. 72). The Philistines are said to have lived as colonists in Crete for a considerable time before their migration to Palestine, but their original home is considered to have been in Asia Minor.

Fig. 57.   Fig. 58a.

Fig. 58b.   Fig. 58c.   Fig. 58d.

CHAPTER V

PRIESTS, MUSICIANS AND MANUAL WORKERS

THE dress of the Egyptian hierarchy was of a simple type when we compare it with that of the Pharaohs, or indeed, with the splendid vestments which have been characteristic of the Christian Church. The chief priest, or prophet, who offered sacrifice in the temple, wore a leopard-skin over his linen robes as did the Pharaoh on similar occasions (*see* Fig. 57, which is after Gardner Wilkinson). These linen garments varied considerably in shape. Sometimes the priests are represented in tight tunics, at other times they have simple robes or draped skirts of linen with a brace over one shoulder, or with the addition of a wide sash round the hips. Again we see a priest offering incense dressed solely in what seems to be rather a clumsy apron fastened with straps round the neck, others again were enveloped in a circular cloak. They seldom wore wigs; shaven heads were general. Fig. 58*a*, *b*, *c* and *d*, illustrates these details of ecclesiastical dress (they are after Gardner Wilkinson). To the Egyptian priesthood marriage was not forbidden and women also were permitted to take part in the ceremonies of religious worship. Plate III (2) (after Gardner Wilkinson) shews a priestess clothed in the ample linen shawl or sari of the New Empire. She carries in her hand three papyrus-flowers (*see also* Chapter VII, Fig. 94*a* and *b*). In Plate III (1) (British Museum) we see Thuthu, wife of Ani the scribe, dressed as a

priestess and holding the sacred systrum, a privilege only permitted to queens, princesses and the wives and daughters
of high priests (*see also* Chapter VII for further references
to Plate III (1)).

Music seems to have pervaded the whole life of the ancient
Egyptians—the temples of the gods, the banqueting halls of
the rich, the street processions and the army on the march,
all had their appropriate music. Among musicians, however,
there is only to a slight degree anything distinctive about
their dress. The royal harpists from the tomb of Rameses III
(*see* Fig. 59, after Champollion) do seem to have a special
costume. The ample robe of the New Empire is here left
to flow loosely round the figure and at the bottom it is
rounded off at each corner to prevent its trailing on the
ground. This costume should be compared with Plate II
and with Fig. 83*a* and *b*.

Feasts were held to the accompaniment of music and
dancing. Fig. 60*a* and *b* (after Gardner Wilkinson) shews a
lady and gentleman of the New Empire in festal costume.
On the head of both there is a cone-shaped lump of perfumed
fat, which would gradually melt over the wig, and also over
the brow of each there hangs a sweet-smelling lotus flower.
The costumes are of the ample gauffered type of the period.
These costumes shewn at Fig. 60*a* and *b* and at 61*a*, *b*, *c* and *d*
should be compared with the explanations of their construction
given in Chapter VII. For example, the shawl or scarf-like
drapery which forms the entire costume of Fig. 60*a* appears
to be arranged after the fashion seen at Fig. 98*a*. In 98*a*,
however, it is the right arm and not the left which is free of
all covering and this is the usual mode, for the obvious
reason that it permits of greater freedom of movement for the
right hand and arm. It is quite possible that the artist who

Fig. 59.

painted Fig. 60*a* sacrificed truth of representation to decorative effect, for in a fresco of the same subject where ladies, similarly dressed, are facing in the opposite direction, we see the right arm free and the left draped in a costume otherwise identical. Fig. 60*b* is wearing the well-known robe seen at Plate I (3) and in the diagrammatic explanation of this Plate given at Fig. 85. Again at Fig. 61*a*, *b*, *c* and *d*, we see this robe worn hanging loose after the fashion seen at Plate II, the explanation of which is again seen at Figs. 83*a* and *b*. Further compare with Fig. 61*a*, *b*, *c* and *d*, the costume of the Royal Harper at Fig. 59 and they will be seen to be almost identical. In effect, this mode of wearing the robe is a popular arrangement for the musician of both sexes.

Fig. 61 (after Champollion) shews a quartette of women musicians of the New Empire, each clad in a full robe of the thinnest and most diaphanous type and each has the perfumed fat and lotus blossom on her head. The four different instruments here represented the advanced state of the art of music at this time. Much has been written by Egyptologists upon this subject of music, and among other authors may be mentioned the name of Gardner Wilkinson in this connection.

There are many representations of workers, both outdoor and indoor, in the Egyptian tomb paintings — agriculturists, fishermen, builders, potters, metal workers, weavers, spinners and domestic servants, to name but a few. Figs. 7 to 11 illustrate certain of these workers of the remote period of the Old Kingdom, yet one thousand years later there is little change in their counterparts of that day, and this changelessness of fashion remains until the end of the days of the New Empire. Fig. 62*a* and *b* (after Gardner Wilkinson) shews

Fig. 60a. Fig. 60b.

a. b. c. d.
Fig. 61.

two women making thread with the spindle, while at Fig. 63*a* and *b* (from the same source) two other women sit at

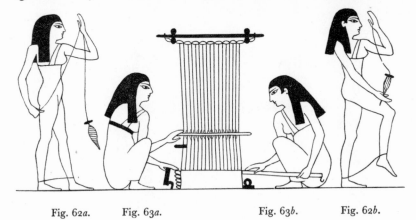

Fig. 62*a*.   Fig. 63*a*.   Fig. 63*b*.   Fig. 62*b*.

the loom.   The costume of these four women workers is the usual tight, breast-to-ankle, tunic, but instead of the usual two straps or braces here there seems to be only one strap in each case, possibly to give greater freedom to the arm. Fig. 64 (after Champollion, who gives its origin as from Thebes, Kourna) shews two women servants who are welcoming guests to the house of their mistress.   Here we see the two domestics wearing not a wig but their natural hair, and clad in the full robe which is draped up in a fashion described at p. 82.   Figs. 64 and 87 should be here compared.)

Figs. 65 to 68 shew various working-class costumes of the New Empire.   Fig. 65 is after Prisse d'Avennes and described by him as being from the Acropolis at Thebes and of the 18th Dynasty.   This man's hair is white and he is a silver-smith.   The kilt as worn by him is probably of that simple type which consisted of a rectangular piece of linen, wrapped

Fig. 64a.   Fig. 64b.

Fig. 65.   Fig. 66.

round the hips, open and slightly overlapping in front.   It appears to have been kept in place by a girdle, though in Fig. 65 the drawing of the Egyptian artist seems to suggest that the top edge of the garment is reinforced by a band, of which a portion shews extending downwards towards the right thigh and emphasizing the overlapping edge.   In Figs. 12 to 16, frontispiece to Vol. II (Gardner Wilkinson), there are representations which give the impression of a band attached to the upper edge while in the same volume at p. 316, cut 437, we see a man stooping, and here the small downward portion referred to is clearly indicating the hanging end of a girdle.   The girdle with hanging ends is the more probable solution.   Fig. 66 (from the same source) is a builder.   One can notice here that the peculiar conventional drawing of the Egyptian artists gives the impression that the kilt is open at the side and has the pendant piece in that position.   This is not so, the man's girdle is tied in the centre of his waist in front, and we are also intended to see the opening of his kilt and its pendant in the same position. It is possible that this pendant which so often appears with this type of kilt may be, in the case of Fig. 66, really a part of the whole garment which has been folded over inwards so as to hang down inside.   In this case the entire kilt might possibly be of segmental shape.   It will be remembered that the segmental shape in garments was known to the ancient Etruscans, who passed it on to the Romans where it became known as the toga, a very large and voluminous drapery which may still have been related in cut to the small plain kilt as shewn at Fig. 66.   Fig. 67 Prisse d'Avennes describes as being from Tell-el-Amarna and of the 18th Dynasty.   It is the figure of a groom holding the reins of the horses of the royal chariot.   He wears a long kilt, formed from a rect-

Fig. 67.   Fig. 68.

angular piece of linen, which is drawn up from behind in characteristic Egyptian fashion, the ends crossed over and allowed to fall down in front. Fig. 68 (origin as 65 and 66) is a land-surveyor. Here we have a worker of superior rank, and in addition to the kilt he wears a small and abbreviated robe of transparent linen over it. This robe is cut in precisely the same manner as the voluminous robes already illustrated and referred to in Chapter VII where their construction is explained.

Fig. 69 is after Rosellini, who describes it as the figure of a fan-bearer to Rameses III and from Ibsamboul. This high official of the court is dressed in the full robe of the period, though, as was occasionally the case, the Egyptian artist has not represented the garment with any great accuracy. This inaccuracy is referred to again and explained fully at Fig.

Fig. 69.

84*a* and *b* in Chapter VII. Over the robe in Fig. 68 is a species of corselet, possibly of quilted and padded linen, whose shape suggests a derivation from the leopard-skin worn as a ceremonial garment, as at Fig. 57. In the tomb of Tut-ankh-amen several fans, similar to that in this illustration, were found—some of these with the feathers almost intact, of which there are excellent photographs in Mr. Howard Carter's book.

Reference has already been made to the custom of wearing the natural hair in place of the usual wigs by women mourners. Fig. 70*a* and *b* (after Champollion, from Thebes, Kourna) shews two of these women. Fig. 70*a* wears what may well be the long full robe of the period, though the drawing is rather vague and it is quite possible that both 70*a* and 70*b* may be clad alike in a species of rectangular

Fig. 70.

a.   b.

shawl girded round the waist to form a skirt and in the case of 70*a* supplemented by a shoulder-cape as seen at Plate I (4). One feels here that this drawing has been executed chiefly with the intention of expressing emotion, not, as in the case of the costume of a great Pharaoh, to add to majesty by richness of ornament and the accurate representation of splendid garments.

The tailpiece of this Chapter, Fig. 71, is after Champollion, who describes it as being from the tomb of Meneptaph at Beni Hassan-el-Quadim and of the 19th Dynasty. The acrobatics here depicted almost suggest a scene in a modern ballet. The costume calls for little comment. The men wear only a girdle with pendant and the tunics of the women are more abbreviated than is usual. Possibly these girls are wearing their own hair, which is plaited into three tight little pigtails—a coiffure which would certainly keep tidy in spite of the most strenuous exertions. In another painting, girls playing a ball game have their hair dressed in similar fashion.

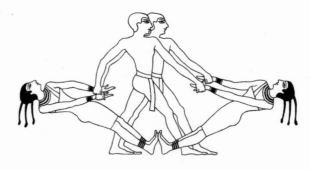

Fig. 71.

CHAPTER VI

FOREIGNERS AS DEPICTED BY EGYPTIAN ARTISTS

EGYPTOLOGISTS are not always unanimous in assigning the countries of origin to the various figures of foreigners which have been portrayed by the Egyptians. There is one case, indeed, in which the earlier writers could not have recognized the men of Crete, whose racial characteristics can now be clearly identified by later authors who have had the advantage of being familiar with the discoveries of Sir Arthur Evans in that island. Most of the earlier authors have described the Cretans as " Asiatics."

Fig. 72 (after Champollion) shews one of a procession of men, similarly clad, who are bearing gifts to the Pharaoh. They were painted on the walls of the tomb of Rekhmire, the vizier of Thuthmosis III (18th Dynasty). Modern writers describe the procession as that of " the reception of Minoan ambassadors (' Keftie ') from Crete." In Vol. II of the series of works on costume, of which the present book is Vol. I, the Cretan costume is fully described and illustrated by drawings from the works of ancient Cretan artists. If these Cretan drawings be compared with Fig. 72, this latter picture may well fill us with admiration for the accurate observation of the Egyptian artist, who in his drawing reproduced so skilfully the costume and the physical characteristics of a foreigner. The very long wavy hair, the

Fig. 72.

decorated kilt with its padded belt and the elaborate foot-
gear, are all depicted with spirit and truthfulness. Even the
vase which this man is carrying is correctly given and of true
Cretan shape.

Fig. 73a, b and c are after Champollion, who states that
they are from Thebes, Biban-el-Molouk, period of Menepthah
I (19th Dynasty), and that the painting from which they are
taken illustrates the Egyptian conception of the " Four
Races of the World," namely, the Egyptian, Africans,
Asiatics and Europeans. Fig. 73a has a Semitic profile, and

a.   *b.*   *c.*   *d.*

Fig. 73.

his embroidered tasselled kilt has affinities with western Asiatic dress. Fig. 73*b* is, of course, an African negro. Fig. 73*c* is represented with a fair skin and blue eyes, with his beard coloured red. Possibly he is intended for a European, though he is also said to be an inhabitant of some part of Western Asia far to the north of Egypt. His arms and legs appear to be tattooed, and over a short girded kilt or loin-cloth he is clad in a cloak of dappled bull's hide which is bound with a band of woven material tying in a knot on the shoulder. A fellow-countryman in the same painting has the striped hide of a wild animal for his cloak and in his case the shoulder-tie is composed of the skin of the legs and paws. The feather head-dress is distinctive. Gardner Wilkinson tells us that the Egyptian name for these people was " the Rebo " and that they were evidently a people of some consequence, " being selected as the type representative of Asia or of the nations of the East in the tomb of the Kings at Thebes."

Fig. 73*d* is another drawing after Champollion, who describes it as being from the tomb of Rameses IV (20th Dynasty). Here we have the representation of an Asiatic in a richly embroidered shawl-drapery, which recalls the Assyrian sculptures with which it should be compared.

Fig. 74*a* and *b*, after Champollion, and from a tomb at Beni-Hassan (12th Dynasty), shews a man and a woman captive in richly patterned woven garments, which are possibly tunics cut on the rectangular plan with a side slit for the left arm. For greater freedom of movement, the right arm and shoulder are completely bared. The rectangle which, as has been said, forms the plan of the garment, has a large slit at the top, which allows for a neck-opening as well as for the emergence of the right arm. The colouring of the man's dress is as follows : ground, red ; chevron-shaped stripes, blue ; vertical stripes, white. The ground of the woman's dress is also red and the pattern, again, is blue and white. Prisse d'Avennes describes these captives as being " of a white race and from their features, together with the spears and lyre carried by others of their fellow-countrymen in this painting, to have been akin to the race depicted on the earliest Greek vases."

Fig. 75 is a drawing after Champollion, who describes it as being " from the tombs at Thebes, Kourna—Asiatics bringing humble tribute to Egypt." Men in similar costume are described in the *Cambridge Ancient History* as being " Syrians from Tunifs."

Fig. 74a.

Fig. 74b.

Fig. 75.

THE COSTUME OF THE HITTITES

The Hittites are frequently represented in Egyptian tomb-paintings, but their costume can better be explained from the sculptures which the Hittites themselves have executed in their own country.

Compared with that magnificent contribution to the world's art which the Egyptians have left to us, that of the Hittites is scant, poor and rude. Nor do we possess, as in the case of Egypt and Assyria, an immense, long-continued volume of scholarship and literature devoted to its arch-aeology. This study and its bibliography is of comparatively recent date.

The Hittite remains, as has been said, consist of sculpture, and that in relief. Some of the later sculptures shew a costume which is an obvious copy of Assyrian dress, but the earlier styles have national characteristics of a quaint and interesting type.

Figs. 76a, b and c shew three Hittite warriors. Fig. 76a is a youth or beardless man from Boghaz-Keni, dating *circa* early thirteenth century, B.C. In this, the most notable features are the tall cone-shaped head-dress decorated in front with hanging metal rings, the hair in a plaited pig-tail and the high boots with their turned-up toes. Fig. 76b is another Hittite soldier in somewhat similar dress. This is from Sinjerli, and is dated *circa* eighth century, B.C. Here we see a different type of head-dress and a shield which has a slight resemblance to those borne by the Cretan warriors. The tunic, belt and wrap-round kilt are the same as those worn by Fig. 76a, and the pig-tail, though shorter, is also

Fig. 76a.   Fig. 76b.   Fig. 76c.

similar.   Fig. 76c still wears the Hittite pigtail, tunic, kilt
and boots, but his plain high cap is not unlike a type worn
in Persia and Mesopotamia.   This is from a sculptured relief
at Carchemish, dating *circa* 900 B.C.

Figs. 77a and c are examples of Hittite women's dress and
Fig. 77b is held by some authorities to be a woman warrior,
the origin of one of those famous " Amazons " with whom
the Greeks have made us familiar.   Other authorities,
however, describe Fig. 77b as " the Hittite War-God."
Fig. 77a is from Boghaz-Keni, *circa* thirteenth century B.C.
and from the same sculptured frieze as Fig. 76a.   Here at
Fig. 77a is the figure of a goddess who leads a procession of
priestesses in similar costume.   It is difficult indeed to arrive
at a correct estimate of the cutting-out or shaping of this
dress.   Probably the skirt is a separate garment, because
there are several women in this same piece of sculpture who

wear an identical skirt and belt, the upper part of their
bodies being either nude or covered with a tight-fitting
short-sleeved vest.   Yet in front of Fig. 77a there hangs a
piece of drapery which suggests that it may be that the entire
costume is really intended by a somewhat unskilful artist to
represent the " sari " type of dress draped over a tight vest
or tunic ; on the other hand, the made-up skirt was well
known as an article of women's dress in the not-so-far-distant
island of Crete from very early times.   The left arm of the
figure may be either enveloped in part of a draping shawl or
" sari," or again it may be that it is covered by a sleeve.
We must leave the make-up of this costume to conjecture
and be content with an accurate observation of the silhouette.
Fig. 77b, the " Amazon " or " War God," forms part of a
bas-relief which adorned the entrance of the palace at
Boghaz-Keni.   One authority gives the date of the sculpture as 1375 B.C., another assigns it to *circa* 1500 B.C.   The
helmet is Assyrian in type and the body is clad in what
appears to be a hauberk of mail.   The legs are slightly
damaged in the sculpture, but they give the impression of
being nude, not booted as are the other Hittite figures
here illustrated.

Fig. 77c is that of a priestess wearing a high tiara, over
which is thrown a veil. A small curling plait of hair appears
in front of the ear, and judging from another female costume
in this series of sculptures, which shews the hair uncovered,
she has the usual Hittite pig-tail at the back under her veil.
Her long fringed tunic is distinctly Assyrian in type.   The
sculpture is from Malatia and the date uncertain.

The technical descriptions of the cutting-out or construction of Ancient Egyptian costume which follow in
Chapter VII have not been attempted in the case of the

Fig. 77a.　　　　　Fig. 77b.　　　　　Fig. 77c.

Hittite styles. The only solution of this constructive aspect of the dress here offered is that of a suggested comparison with the explanation given of the construction of Egyptian, Assyrian and Persian costume.

6

THE CONSTRUCTION OR SHAPING OF ANCIENT EGYPTIAN COSTUME

THE garments about to be described have been illustrated in previous chapters, their dates and the place of their wearers in the social scheme having been given. We may now consider the costumes from their constructional or technical aspect. As has been said, for men's dress the most frequently worn of all Egyptian garments was the kilt, usually of linen, often stiffened and as a rule rectangular in shape. It varied considerably in size, at times merely a short loin-cloth, in other cases reaching to the ankles and assuming the proportions of a skirt. The kilt also shews variations in its method of adjustment. The simplest examples were of the " wrap-round " variety, other styles were drawn tightly round the loins at the back and allowed to fall over a girdle in front with the effect of a cascade as, for example, Fig. 67, p. 61. In a voluminous type such as Fig. 68 the linen was usually thinner and gauffered. This practice of drawing up the material at the back and allowing it to fall over a girdle in front was probably the origin of a two-piece kilt formed of what may have been a semicircular garment at the back and sides and a small apron in the shape of an isosceles triangle filling up the gap in front—the triangle standing upon its apex as at Fig. 45, p. 40, where we see the carefully gauffered kilt of the Pharaoh with the semicircular part crossed over and the triangular apron hanging from underneath. In other cases we see the triangular portion standing on its base (*see* Fig. 23), and at Fig. 54 we see again the triangular part on its apex and worn outside the main part of the kilt. Here this triangular apron has every appearance of having been padded and stiffened so as to form defensive armour for the soldier who wears it. It will be remembered that the kilt of the Pharaoh was in most cases enriched by the magnificent pendant or apron hanging down in front, of which numerous illustrations have been given.

While the kilt, as worn by men, varied in its silhouette and proportions, the breast-high, ankle-length tunic with its characteristic braces, varied little. The favourite garment for women's wear in Ancient Egypt varies little if at all in shape from the period of the Old Kingdom dynasties to the latest dynasty of the New Empire, and it is also remarkable as being worn by women of all ranks. Plate I is an example of the tunic of which there are also several illustrations in previous chapters. For the complete head-dress of this costume, *see* Fig. 78. The plate itself is a representation of the goddess Mut or Mouth ; it is a drawing after Champollion and the date is *c*. 700 B.C.

Fig. 78 shews the goddess wearing, over the hawk head-dress of Isis, the Double Crown of Upper and Lower Egypt (the " Pshent "), which has been omitted perforce from the plate owing to lack of space. In her right hand she carries the Flower-Sceptre characteristic of a goddess, and in her left hand she holds the Ankh. The painted decoration on her tunic repeats the motif of the head-dress. A drawing of this costume upon a lay figure, together with the plan of the same as a flat pattern, are given at Fig. 79*a*

Fig. 78.

and *b*.   Figs. 80*a* and *b* and Figs. 81*a* and *b* were worn by
both sexes.   Fig. 80, the tunic with short sleeves, is illustrated
in wear by Gardner Wilkinson on a terra-cotta statuette
(Vol. II, p. 334), and this was not on the whole a common
type of tunic amongst the Egyptians, though in other countries
it has been in use since very early times, its simple T-shaped
plan being the foundation of many styles of costume from
Asia and in later days also from Europe.   Fig. 81*a* and *b*,
which is a sleeveless tunic, though again not of frequent
occurrence in Ancient Egypt, yet is seen in wear by certain
Egyptians as far back as the days of the Old Kingdom.
Plate I (2) shews an interesting variant of the usual type of
braced tunic.   This example widens out at the bottom and
its braces are narrower than is usual.   The drawing is after
Rosellini, who describes the figure as being that of Queen
Cleopatra-Coccia and from the temple at Philae.   The

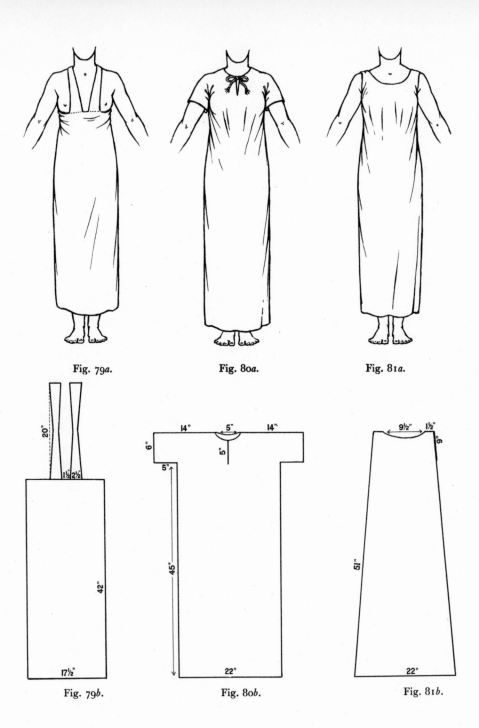

Fig. 79a.

Fig. 80a.

Fig. 81a.

Fig. 79b.

Fig. 80b.

Fig. 81b.

queen here is seen in the costume of a goddess and in the original drawing she wears the feathers and disk of Hathor. This tall head-dress has been omitted, for lack of space, from Plate II, but it is illustrated at Fig. 39, p. 35 in the costume of Queen Ankhnes Neferatra.   The tunic worn in Plate I (2) widens out at the bottom, most probably after the simple scheme shewn at Fig. 82, p. 78, so that the *appearance* of a swathed drapery shewn in the illustration is simply a painted *striped decoration* having as its inspiration the favourite Egyptian mode of draping, *i.e.* the material tightly stretched across the loins at the back and drawn up towards the front as is seen in innumerable examples of Egyptian costume. (*See also* Fig. 90.)

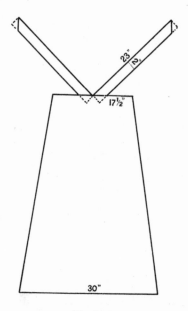

Fig. 82.

We now come to that voluminous robe which became popular in Egypt during the 18th Dynasty, and is characteristic of the costume of the New Empire. This robe has been illustrated in wear in previous chapters. Among other examples see Figs. 34, 40 and 59. Plate II and Fig. 59 shew this simple rectangular dress hanging free with its shape plainly visible, but it is far otherwise with the more elaborately draped examples where the cut or shape is completely disguised by the arrangement on the figure. At times, as has been said, the bottom corners were rounded off to prevent its dragging on the ground when worn loose and ungirded (*see* again the Royal Harper at Fig. 59). The other loosely hanging example (shewn at Plate II) has for its subject the god Osiris with his characteristic head-dress composed of the tall White Crown of Upper Egypt supported by tall white plumes on either side, this arrangement is called by some, but not by all, Egyptologists the " Atef Crown." In his hands he carries the ceremonial crook and flail and wears the ceremonial curved beard of the gods. To make the somewhat archaic drawing of Plate II quite clear reference should be made to Figs. 83*a* and *b*. In the former the robe is shewn draped on a lay figure and in the latter we have a flat pattern of the same. Several actual specimens of this type of robe have been preserved to us. One is illustrated in *Aegyptische Monumenten* by Dr. C. Leemans, the original being in the Leyden Museum. Similar in shape to Fig. 83*b* this specimen is tied at the neck with little tasselled cords, has a fringe at the bottom and ornamental stitchery down each side. Sir Gardner Wilkinson illustrates a robe with a corded decoration sewn round the neck and wrist apertures and with a heavy fringe at the bottom. Lastly, Mr. Howard Carter in his book on Tut-ankh-amen

Fig. 83a.   Fig. 83b.

(Vol. III) shews a photograph of an actual robe—one of
two specimens found in the tomb.   In this the decoration is
of wool tapestry and its arrangement, though not its detail,
corresponds almost exactly with those numerous examples of
the Egypto-Roman Period (the so-called " Coptic Grave-
clothes ") which are exhibited in the Victoria and Albert
Museum, London, and elsewhere.   In Vol. II of this series
of the *Technical History of Costume* there are several illustrations
of these Egypto-Roman tunics.

Next we come to various methods of draping this robe
as worn by the Egyptians and here comparison should be
made with the same garment draped as " The Royal Robe

of Persia " at Plate IX, where the effect sought after is so
entirely different from that which became the vogue in
Egypt.   Plate I (3) is an illustration of " Ani the Scribe "
taken from the *Book of the Dead* (British Museum), 1450 B.C.
Here we get an elaborate and characteristically Egyptian
method of draping.   In Plate II the edges of the robe are
sewn together down each side, leaving only enough of an
opening for the hands, but in Plate I (3) it is left open at each
side and the front half of the garment is taken and pinned
at the back of the waist, while the back half is drawn towards
the front and girded with a wide sash, measuring about
32 inches by 120 inches.   In depicting this form of drapery
the Egyptian artist often found himself in difficulties with the
perspective of the folds of the material, hence he often draws
the robe as if it had one sleeve and one open side.   The
artist's effort to draw Fig. 84a and b illustrates the point in
question.   They are both intended for the same costume seen
in different positions ; while the robe is clearly represented at
Fig. 84a, in Fig. 84b there appears to be a sleeve.   These

Fig. 84a.   Fig. 84b.

two drawings are after Rosellini, who describes them as being from Beit Qualli, in Nubia, dating sixteenth century B.C. Continuing the description of Plate I (3), reference should be made to Fig. 85, which is a drawing of this costume cut out and draped on a lay figure. After the back and front of the robe have been arranged as described on p. 81 the wide girdle or sash is draped as follows : Commence at the right side of waist, drawing the sash downwards towards the left and round the hips at the back, next draw upwards across the front from right to left and round the hips at the back, next draw upwards across the front from right to left and round the waist at the back and tuck in the remaining length of sash in front as shewn in Fig. 85. Fig. 86a, b and c is drawn from the lay figure on which has been draped the same arrangement of this robe but with the sash differently adjusted as shewn. It is taken from a British Museum sculpture in the round, dating 2500 B.C. Fig. 87a and b is from the Cairo Museum and represents an Egyptian priest or religious official of 1300 B.C. In this case there is no girdle or sash. The front of the robe is first pinned behind the waist and then the back part is drawn forward, caught up and tucked in in front of the waist as shewn. Fig. 64, p. 59, shewing two women house-servants, is not depicted with any great clearness by the Egyptian artist, but, as far as can be gathered, the draping here is the same as at Fig. 87.

There was a method of draping which was specially characteristic of the dress of women. Plate III (1) is taken from the *Book of the Dead* (British Museum), 1450 B.C. and represents Thuthu, the wife of Ani the Scribe dressed as a priestess and holding the systrum. Fig. 88 shews her robe draped upon a lay figure. In this case the front half is *not* pinned behind

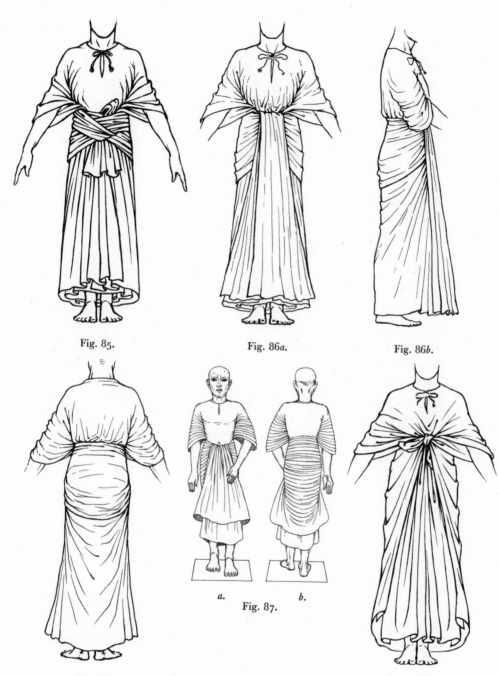

Fig. 85.

Fig. 86a.

Fig. 86b.

Fig. 86c.

a.   Fig. 87.   b.

Fig. 88.

the back of the waist but is kept quite full in front, and the back half, instead of being girded by a sash, is drawn round to the front and the edges tied up in a knot, high up, just below the breast. At times this robe, on women, is not knotted under the breast but, instead, it is kept in place by a high girdle of the type shewn at Plate I (4), which plate introduces us to another form of garment. This, though not of very frequent occurrence, characterizes some of the women's costumes of the New Empire. It seems to have consisted of a skirt and a cape. The drawing is after Rosellini, who gives its origin as being from " the Valley of the Queens " at Thebes and as representing " the Queen Amon-mai, wife of Thuthmosis II (18th Dynasty)." We have already seen a kind of cape illustrated as part of a 12th Dynasty man's costume at Fig. 20, p. 17, which has a rectangular piece of material thrown round the shoulders and fastened at the two corners in front. The cape of Queen Amon-mai is differently adjusted and a solution of the method is offered at Fig. 89a ; here the shape, as will be seen, is rectangular. To drape it, take the corners *a* and *e* and twist the material until the triangles *a b c* and *d e f* each becomes like a twisted cord, then knot as shewn at Fig. 89d. The skirt is also

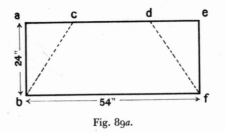

Fig. 89a.

rectangular in shape (*see* Fig. 89c). It is seamed down the short sides of the rectangle. A narrow strip of material is

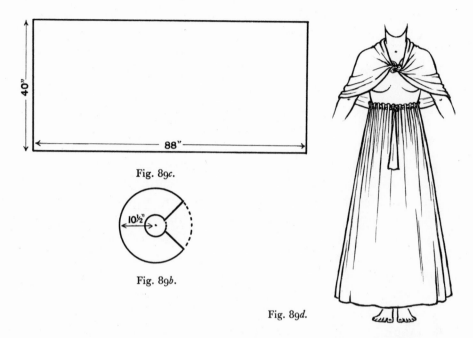

Fig. 89c.

Fig. 89b.

Fig. 89d.

threaded through at the waist-line to form a gathering-string which is pulled in and knotted round the waist (*see* Fig. 89d). Over this is worn a narrow girdle about a hundred inches in length which passes twice round the waist, leaving long ends to hang down in front. As has been said, this girdle was also worn to keep the robe, shewn at Plate III (1), in position, as an alternative to the knotted edges. See also Fig. 40 after Champollion, who describes the drawing as " an Egyptian Princess from the Palace of Rameses IV at Medinet Habu with characteristic costume and insignia." Fig. 90 shews another method of wearing a similarly cut skirt, especially as seen in the latest periods of the New Empire. In this case there is no waist-cord, instead two pieces of the upper edge, about half a yard apart, are taken in the hands and twisted ; one is then crossed over the other and tucked inside, afterwards the other is pulled up and forms an " ear," as shewn in sketch. This particular type of draping is worn at the present day by both men and women in Burma and called " the Sarong." This draping should be compared with Plate I (2) where it gives the inspiration of the painted, striped decoration on the dress of Queen Cleopatra-Coccia. Fig. 89b is a flat pattern of the deep, jewelled collar shewn in wear at Plate I (4) and forming such a feature of the dress of persons of distinction in Egypt. It was fastened at the back of the neck by the tying of two small strings attached or, at times, there was a jewelled clasp. Often the corners at the back were rounded off with the latter method of fastening. Figs. 91, 92 and 93 are taken from British Museum sculptured figures. Fig. 91 is that of an Egyptian woman which dates 1450 B.C. Here we have the skirt cut as at Fig. 90, to which is added a long rectangular cloak. The top edge of this skirt in Fig. 91 is gathered up in the hands as in Fig. 90, and crossed over in the first stage of making a knot. The two corners of the cloak are then laid upon it and the knot completed so as to hold the cloak in place. This is made clear in the drawing. Fig. 92, which dates A.D. 200, shews a Roman adaptation of the same costume. The figure wears, underneath, the ordinary Roman woman's costume (the " Stola ") which is of a sleeveless type. Over the Stola, which it holds in at the waist, is worn an Egyptian skirt to which is knotted a small rectangular scarf, forming a little cape over the shoulders, as shewn in the drawing. Fig. 93a is a Greek costume of the fourth century B.C. in which again the Egyptian influence is strongly marked. To knot the cloak to the over-skirt in this last example the fullness of the skirt should be bunched up

Fig. 90.

Fig. 91.

Fig. 92.

Fig. 93a.

Fig. 94a.

Fig. 93b.

in one hand, the two corners of the cloak should be taken in the other hand and formed into a loop. Then, when the bunched-up piece of skirt is passed through the loop, the latter should then be drawn tight, as at Fig. 93*a*. Fig. 93*b*, which supplements the diagrammatic drawing at 93*a* (which diagram has been adapted from an original now in the British Museum) is a representation of a Graeco-Roman statue of the goddess Isis (now in the Capitoline Museum, Rome). Fig. 93*b* is here given because the power of representing drapery in a realistic fashion, which was possessed by the sculptors of this Graeco-Roman age, enables the costume to be well understood ; whereas the very beautiful but stiff and archaic Egyptian sculpture of a similar dress is difficult to grasp as a piece of constructive drapery.

We now come to a completely different type of dress, though at first glance when seen in the Egyptian paintings and sculptures it appears very similar to the Robe. This garment may be called the Shawl or " Sari " type of dress as its measurements, shape and draping are almost identical with the Indian woman's Sari. In Egyptian costume it is also essentially a garment for women, and like the Robe it is characteristic of the New Empire. There can be no doubt of the Eastern origin of this garment.* It is found in Egyptian costume after the date of the Hyksos invasion with its resultant Asiatic influences. See also illustrations of the Mesopotamian Section of this volume where we see it in wear in the " Land of Elam " as early as the second millenium B.C. Fig. 38 representing Queen Taia (18th Dynasty) and Fig. 39, Queen Ankhnes Neferatra (26th Dynasty) are seen to be wearing this costume. See also Plate III (2) after Gardner

---

* Maspero refers to it as Assyrian dress when describing the statue of Amophis III in Egypt, p. 166.

PLATE II

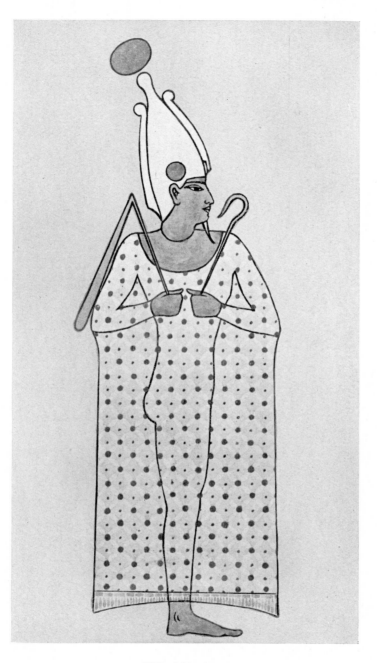

THE GOD OSIRIS

PLATE III

2. ANCIENT EGYPTIAN PRIESTESS

1. THUTHU, WIFE OF ANI

Wilkinson, who describes the wearer as "the sister of a priest" (from Thebes). Figs. 94 *a* and *b* are shewn to explain the exact manner of draping and cutting out the costume at Plate III (2) which is, however, only one of the various methods of arranging the Sari. Fig. 94*b* is draped as follows :

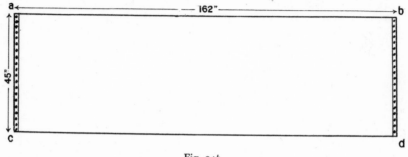

Fig. 94*b*.

Take the garment (which should measure about 162 inches by 45 inches) and first tie a cord round the waist and tuck into it corner *b* at left-hand side of waist, pass edge *b* around the back and round the right side to front again, then gather up some of the material into pleats and tuck them into the centre front of waist-cord ; now pass round the back again to right side ; catch up the whole drapery and throw it upwards from right-hand side of waist under the left armpit, pass on round the back and over the right shoulder towards the front, then throw the remaining portion of garment across the chest and backwards over the left shoulder ; take corner *a* and bring it round under the right armpit, release corner *b* which was first tucked in to waist-cord and tie it to corner *a*. The corner *c* will hang down at the back and the corner *d* will appear at the bottom hem beside the left ankle.

The ingenuity displayed in the draping of these garments can best be realized when one actually drapes them upon a

7

lay figure, as has been done in the case of Fig. 94*a* which is drawn from such a model. If this drapery which has been described be compared with a modern arrangement of the Indian Sari the resemblance will be seen to be striking (*see* Figs. 95*b*, *c* and *d*). This Sari, which measures 4½ yards by 39 inches, is shewn at Fig. 95*a*. The method of draping is as

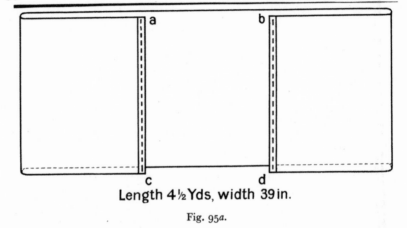

Length 4½ Yds, width 39 in.

Fig. 95*a*.

follows : Tie a waist-cord ; take corner *b* and fix it to the waist-cord at right side of waist then pass the edge *b–a* across the front of waist round the left side towards the back, and round the back of waist again to the right side ; now take up some pleats in the material and tuck them inside the waist-cord in centre front of waist, then pass on the drapery round the waist to back and round to the right side again. Now catch up all the remaining drapery and throw it upwards across the chest over the left shoulder. Let the corner *c* hang down at back, and bring the corner *a* round towards the front of waist, pass it over the rest of the drapery to the left side of waist and then tuck it into the waist-cord as seen at Fig. 95*b*. This completes one method of draping the

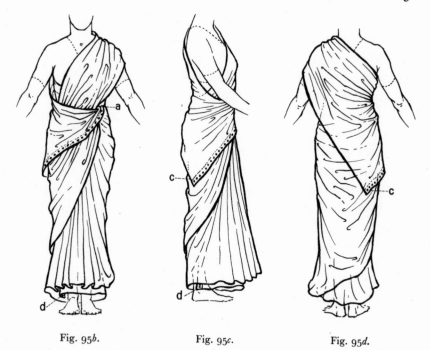

Fig. 95*b*. Fig. 95*c*. Fig. 95*d*.

Indian Sari. The measurements given at Fig. 95*a* will drape it on a woman of 5 feet 4 inches. For a smaller woman the Sari should be narrower. It can, as a rule, be observed that when the Egyptians dealt with this form of drapery, all the folds appear to be designed to radiate from one point, and that usually at the right side of the waist with charming effect. Figs. 96, 97 and 98 are examples of this radiation of folds. They are from the British Museum and of a period late in the New Empire.

To drape Fig. 96 take a piece of material identical with that shewn at Fig. 94*b*. Take the corner *a* and hold it at right side of waist in front, pass the edge *a–b* round the back and round the left side to the front again, tuck in some pleats in centre front and pass round the back to the left side of waist under left arm towards the front ; catch up the entire drapery and throw over right shoulder, pass the upper edge of the garment round the back of the neck and over the left shoulder and downwards across the breast to right, where the corner *b* should be tied to the corner *a*. Corner *d* hangs down in a point at the back and corner *c* (not shewn in diagram) hangs down near the right ankle. This completes the drapery.

To drape Fig. 97*a* take a piece of material measuring 182 inches by 45 inches. Tie a waist-cord and hold the corner *a* at left side of waist in front, then throw the whole garment upwards over the right shoulder to the back ; take the corner *c*, bring it round under the right arm and hold it together with the corner *a* ; draw the edge *a–b* (which still hangs over the right shoulder) downwards across the back to left side of waist. Bring it round to front of waist and pin it to the corners *a* and *c* at the left side of waist in front, passing the garment on round the front ; form a few pleats in the centre front and tuck into waist-cord, then pass it round the right side of waist and upwards across the back, over the left shoulder, downwards across the breast to the right side of waist ; here pass a loop of material over the left wrist as shewn in diagram ; now pass a girdle round the waist over the entire drapery and knot it at the right side of waist as shewn in the diagram, so confining the drapery as illustrated. The corners *a* and *c* are hidden under superimposed drapery at the left side of waist. The corner *b* appears near the left hand and the corner *d* hangs down near the left ankle. The measurements of the drapery are intended for a woman about 5 feet 6 inches in height, the width of the material should be less than

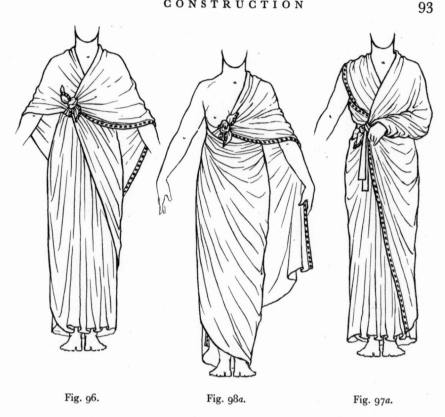

Fig. 96.   Fig. 98a.   Fig. 97a.

45 inches for a smaller person. This completes a very complicated drapery.

(The four beautiful little goddesses, who with outstretched
arms guard the Canopie Chest from the tomb of Tut-ankh-
amen wear the Shawl or Sari costume draped in a fashion not unlike Fig. 96 (*see* Vol. III, Plates VII and VIII,
H. Carter's *Tut-ankh-amen*).

By contrast with the last example Fig. 98*a* is a drapery of
great simplicity, measuring 82 inches by 50 inches. To drape
it proceed as follows : Take the corner *a* of Fig. 98*b* and hold

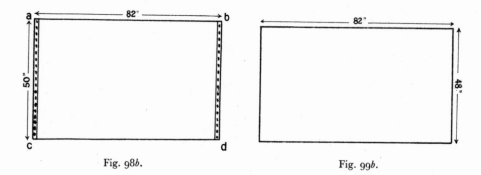

Fig. 98b.   Fig. 99b.

it at right side of waist in front, pass the edge *a–b* round the
back of waist to the left side and across the front of waist,
pass it round to the right side again under the right arm and
towards the back, now upwards over the left shoulder, tie
the corner *a* to the corner *b* in front.   Here *a* and *b* are
knotted together, *d* hangs down from the left hand and *c* is
near the right ankle.   This completes the drapery.   Fig.
99*a* and *b* shews an arrangement of a cloak.   It is worn by a
man and the date is sixth century B.C.   This simple drapery
can be readily understood by a glance at the diagram.
Fig. 100*a* is from a sculpture in the British Museum, No. 565,
18th or 19th Dynasty.   Here are two seated figures, those of
an official and his wife.   The costume of the latter has been
already explained at Fig. 96.   Fig. 100*a* wearing the Robe,
of which garment several illustrations have already been
given.   In Fig. 100*a*, however, we see an example also of the
corselet worn over it and here the corselet is without braces.
It was most probably of either quilted linen or of leather.   An
explanation of its cut or construction is offered at Fig. 100*b*.
It should be added that the man and woman in this sculpture
wear, each of them, the large and stately wigs of the New
Empire over their elegant draperies.   Fig. 101*a* and *b* has

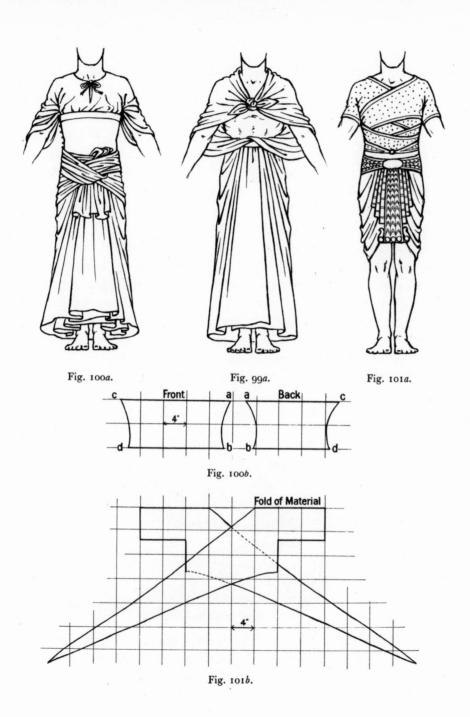

Fig. 100a.

Fig. 99a.

Fig. 101a.

Fig. 100b.

Fig. 101b.

already been referred to at Fig. 45 where it is shewn as part
of the military dress of the Pharaoh, Rameses III. The
" crossover " corselet is worn with different types of kilt and
even over the long robe a kilt of gauffered linen identical in
shape with that in the diagram is worn by Tut-ankh-amen
(Plate VII, Vol. II, H. Carter's *Tut-ankh-amen*). It seems to
be characteristically Egyptian. As will be seen, the kilt in
the diagram Fig. 101*a* differs from the gauffered example
seen at Fig. 45. Fig. 101*b* offers a simple method of cutting
out the " crossover " corselet. Fig. 102 is after Champollion,
who describes it as being a portrait of Ptolemy Philadelphus
(33rd Dynasty). This very late example of Egyptian art is
here shewn as an example of the exaggerated corner of some
types of the fold-over kilt, which from early to late periods
was an occasional feature of this type of garment.

It would seem here as if the usual rectangular cut of the
kilt had been abandoned and the garment narrowed off at
the top so as to have a point somewhat sharper than the

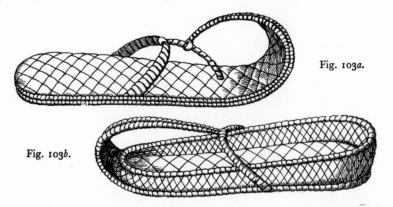

Fig. 103*a*.

Fig. 103*b*.

traditional right angle at the lower edge. That particular
variety of kilt shewn at Fig. 102 is richly decorated and an
enlargement of its detail is given in the next chapter. Sandals

are shewn at Fig. 103a and b. The drawings are after
Gardner Wilkinson, who tells us that these two examples of
footwear are from the Berlin Museum and that Egyptian
sandals were made of woven palm leaves, papyrus stalks
or other similar materials. It will be seen on examining
previous illustrations that on most occasions the Egyptian
went barefooted, and that when sandals are shewn as part
of the costume they are usually the wear of persons of
consequence.

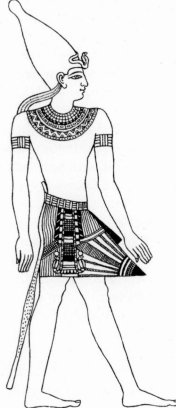

Fig. 102.

CHAPTER VIII

EGYPTIAN ORNAMENT

THERE are few writers on the history of ornament who fail
to give a prominent place to the magnificent and varied
decorations for which Ancient Egypt is justly famous. There
is here a triumph of colour as well as of form, and it takes
either the character of flat painted ornament or that executed
upon sculpture in the round or in low relief. As applied to
costume in particular we have evidences of tapestry-woven
ornament in specimens of actual material which have been
found in the tombs. There is in addition a number of
representations which are evidently those of costumes
enriched with embroidery and with painted decorations. The
Egyptians used their favourite decorative motifs upon temple
walls and ceilings, upon tombs, furniture, chariots, costume
and jewellery alike, or with comparatively slight modification.
It will, therefore, be permissible to discuss their ornament in
the abstract apart from its application. Great collections of
Egyptian ornament were made for the *Histories of Ornament*
produced during the nineteenth century and among those
published during the second and third quarters especially,
there are several large folios illustrated with carefully drawn
lithographs in colour. From these volumes most of the
examples here given are drawn, with the exception of a few
which have been sketched directly from mummy cases in the
British Museum. Plates IV and V have in their detail
strong resemblances one with another, yet the differing

arrangements of their simple elements never fail to give a sense of variety and interest. Perhaps the two most frequently used details are the conventionalized lotus and papyrus. In Plate IV (1), for example, the lotus flower or lotus flower and bud occurs at *a, b* and *c*, while the papyrus is seen in the lowest part of the border at *d*. The decorations at *e* to *k* are purely geometric. A characteristic method of colour-arrangement is shewn at *f* and *g*. The colouring of such decorative borders in the styles of other countries generally exhibits a simple alternation, as, for example, "red-blue, red-blue, etc." In *f* and *g*, however, we find " blue-white, green-white, blue-white, red-white, blue-white, etc." At *g* we have " green-white, red-white, buff-white, blue-white, green-white, etc." These rhythmic colour arrangements are almost always seen in Egyptian ornament in preference to the more usual alternation and this is no doubt the reason why the patterns, childishly simple in form, continue to fascinate and please. Much of the ornament in Plates IV and V will be recognized as having been indicated (necessarily on a very small scale) upon the costumes illustrated in previous chapters, but they can be better appreciated when referred to the examples here drawn to a larger size. In Plate IV (2), besides the lotus ornament at *i, j* and *k*, we have at *a* the famous symbolic design of the sun's disk, supported on either side by uraei and outspread wings. A sense of repose is conveyed by the strongly horizontal arrangement and the idea of protection is suggested by the wings themselves in which the radiation of the feathers by gradual transition from the horizontal to the vertical adds another attractive feature to this immensely impressive design. Those equally beautiful radiating effects given at *b* and *c* at once arrest the eye. Here are seen the sacred emblems of the hawk and the scarabaeus (beetle) respectively, which are met with over and over again in Egyptian costume decorations. Of the two, the hawk is the more frequently used on costume, as has been illustrated in previous chapters, but the scarabaeus is a favourite motif in Egyptian jewellery. There was a pectoral with pendant beetles in lapis lazuli among the treasures found in the tomb of Tut-ankh-amen. At *g* there is a specimen of that feather ornament to which reference has already been made in connection with the corselet of the god Amen-ra at Fig. 26, p. 23. From Plate IV (2), *d, e, f* and *h* are again examples of geometric motifs. In Plate V, Figs. *a* and *b* give two enlargements of that pendant apron, such a frequent and decorative incident of the costumes of the Pharaohs, as will be seen in wear on reference to previous chapters. An actual specimen of one of these pendants has been found in the tomb of Tut-ankh-amen. It consists of plates of gold inlaid with coloured glass and precious stones, the plates being joined together with tiny golden beads. The coloured strips at either side of these royal pendants were most probably of painted or inlaid leather. Again *c* and *d* are two illustrations of the lotus ornament and *e* gives a characteristic treatment of the feather ; it is from a fan and it can be noted that the striped effect here seen is precisely the same as that on the two tall plumes surmounting the head-dress of the god Amen-Ra at Fig. 26.

The question now arises as to how the colouring of these plates of painted ornament conforms to that of the actual ornament upon the materials from which the Egyptian costumes were made. The artists who represented these costumes in colour in ancient times were dependant on a very limited range of paints, and these paints did not necessarily correspond with the dyes used for spun threads

2,4678

or woven materials. Though there seems to be evidence at times that ancient garments were painted as well as dyed, the pigments for application to woven stuff would have had to be specially prepared. Plate I (1) is a case in point, it is most probable that the decoration here shewn was painted. On the other hand, Plate II has the appearance of a printed or woven pattern. A range of the actual, coloured dyes has been preserved for us in those used for the decorations of the Egypto-Roman tunics to which reference has already been made. A list of these dyes in order of preference may be given as follows :

1. Deep warm purple.
2. Indigo blue, deep and medium.
3. Dull madder-red, deep and paler.
4. Dull apple green of medium depth.
5. Dull yellow-orange.

These colours are illustrated from actual examples in the chapter on Roman Costumes in Vol. II of this series of *The Technical History of Costume* (*see* Plate IV).

The habit of wearing gloves, and those of a highly ornamental kind, was not unknown to the Egyptians. In Mr. Howard Carter's book, *Tut-ankh-Amen*, Vol. III, there is a photograph of a pair of linen gloves, the backs of which are closely covered with a decoration in wool tapestry. The design on the backs of these gloves consists of a closely arranged repeating pattern, the details of which consists of lotus buds and flowers alternating. This tapestry decoration was executed in woollen yarns dyed as already described, the main ground being always of linen.

Fig. 104 is a corselet (the drawing is after Rosellini, who describes it as being from the tomb of Rameses IV, first king of the 19th Dynasty, *c.* fifteenth century B.C.). Here we see a diagram of the garment. For the main design a pair of winged quadrupeds and a pair of lions are arranged to face each other and the whole effect has a heraldic appearance. The design is not characteristically Egyptian, but has evidently been adapted from a foreign source. Its colouring, however (as illustrated by Rosellini), and the disposition of its detail suggest that the original was executed in wool tapestry on a linen ground, to which method of decoration reference has already been made.

Fig. 105 *a* to *f* gives further examples of Egyptian decoration. Fig. 105*a* is after Champollion, who describes it as being from the portrait of Rameses IX (20th Dynasty). Here the successive borders are extremely simple in their detail, yet the well-contrasted bands which form the pattern make up an exceedingly pleasing design. Fig. 105*b* and *c* are again from Champollion. These are the details of the collar and kilt of Fig. 102, p. 97. In the collar one of the borders having leaf-tips with veins strikes a somewhat unusual note. The kilt (*c*) is decorated in a manner frequently found on the stiff, triangular fold-overs of this type of garment. It should be realized that the Egyptian artist here intended to convey that the pendant apron should hang down in the centre front and the stiffened part project towards the left side of the figure. Fig. 105*d* is after Rosellini and Owen Jones, the latter giving its origin as from a tomb at Beni-Hassan. This border has as its inspiration the flowering head of the papyrus reed and is called " khaker " ornament. At Fig. 28 the bundle of reeds has been shewn as the central detail of a royal head-dress and its origin explained. See also Fig. 30, p. 25—the same reeded ornament forming the " triple-Atef " or " Hoetas " crown. Fig. 105*e* is after Gardner Wilkinson (Vol. II, p. 346) and is from an Egyptian

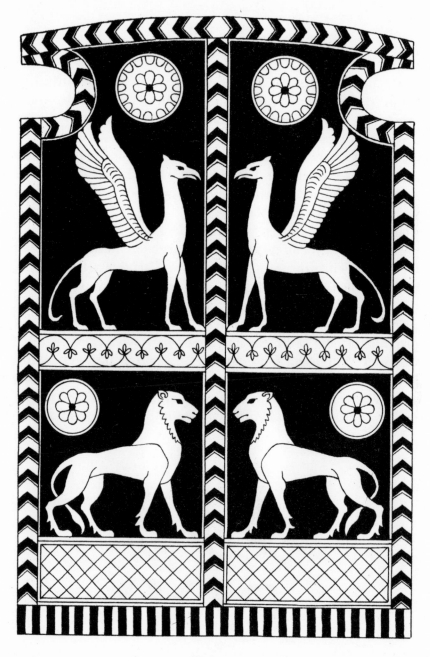

Fig. 104.

lady's hand-mirror. These mirrors were highly burnished metal disks inserted into handles of varied form, some presenting the figure of a woman, others a flower, a column, or even a grotesque head whose ugliness would set off the good looks of the lady reflected above it ; this mirror is from a painted representation at Thebes, though there are many actual specimens of these mirrors in our museums (*see* Gardner Wilkinson, Vol. I, p. 160). Fig. 105*f* is part of a shallow wooden saucer probably designed to hold a small portion of ointment taken from a large jar and is intended for convenience in use at the toilet. This delightful design, with two fish, each holding a spray of lotus, is an example of the principle of balance in design in place of the usual principle of symmetry which pervades most Egyptian ornament. Fig. 106, the tail-piece to this chapter, is after Gardner Wilkinson, who calls it " Egyptian Buffoons," and its origin is Thebes. The reeded head-dress here shewn should be compared with Figs. 105*d* and also Figs. 28 and 30, and is another example of design founded on the papyrus.

Fig. 106.

PLATE IV

ANCIENT EGYPTIAN DECORATION

(1)   (2)

PLATE V

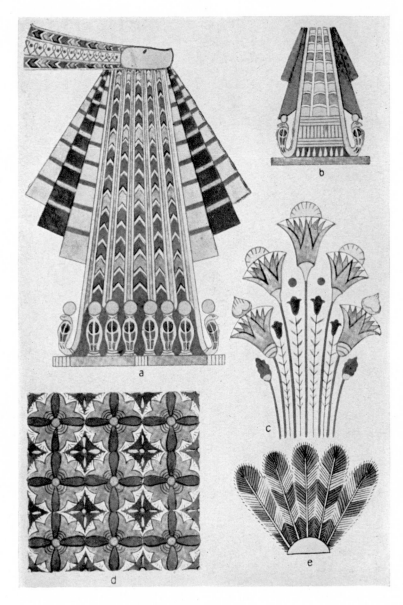

ANCIENT EGYPTIAN ORNAMENT

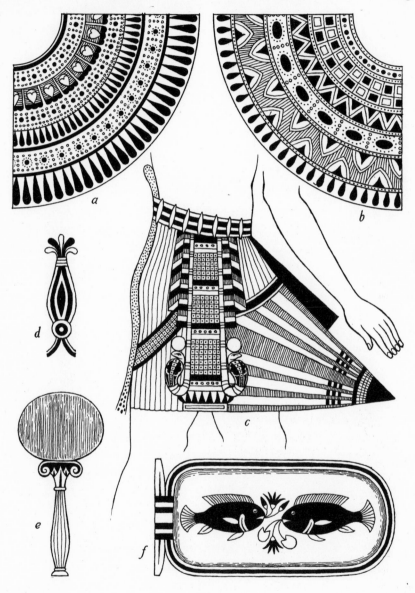

Fig. 105.

8

ANCIENT MESOPOTAMIAN COSTUME

INTRODUCTION

THE costumes in this section can be divided into three distinct types, and their dates (which are here given in round numbers but more exactly with each illustration of costume) are consecutive. The styles are as follows :

1. The sheepskin skirt or kilt, *c.* 3000 B.C.
2. The large shawl or drapery, *c.* 2000 B.C.
3. The tunic with or without an added shawl or shawls, *c.* 1000 B.C.–700 B.C.

In Style 1. There is little difference between the dresses of the men and women ; while military dress, except for the weapons carried, does not differ greatly from that of civilians.

In Style 2. The drapery of the shawl differs among men and women. The military dress is short and trim, differing much from the civilian dress of ceremony. Throughout this style we have a survival of *Style 1* in that the costumes of gods and goddesses are made of a woven material which imitates the fleece of the sheep.

In Style 3. We have a far more advanced and developed costume. As in most Asiatic countries the dress of the men seems more important than that of the women. Military costume is highly specialized, shewing armour. Lavish ornament is characteristic of the more elaborate civilian dresses.

While there is a certain amount of overlapping among these three styles, we can on the whole associate them with three great names prominent in Mesopotamian history and at the same time with three geographical regions of that country.

1. We can, for example, associate *Style 1* with the *Sumerian* peoples of *Southern* Mesopotamia.

2. We can also associate *Style 2* with the *Babylonian* peoples and with *Middle* Mesopotamia, though *Style 2* is seen in wear in the later Sumerian era (*see* Fig. 117a).

3. Lastly, we can associate *Style 3* with the *Assyrians* of *Northern* Mesopotamia, though here again we find *Style 3* in wear in the later Babylonian era (*see* Fig. 128a and b).

CHAPTER IX

SUMERIAN STYLE IN COSTUME

THIS civilization was already old before the third millenium B.C. ; but the dress remained primitive compared with the progress in other arts, such as working in metal, for example.

The dress consisted of a sheepskin skirt with slit opening or more probably a kilt of the wrap-round variety and was as a rule kept in place by a padded belt. In some cases the material of the garment was of sufficient length to be passed upwards under the belt and a short end of it was thrown from behind forwards over the left shoulder. There are examples of the kilt without the fleece, but usually the whole of the sheep's wool was left on the skin. This is represented in a highly conventionalized and primitive style, but the fact that the fleece of an actual sheep, on the animal's back, is represented by Sumerian artists in an identical manner leaves no doubt in the mind that the Sumerians at the commencement of the third millenium B.C. were clothed in sheepskins, though it is possible that the fleeces may have been combed and trimmed so giving the flounced effect. The other details of these costumes will be best explained by the drawings here following. The so-called " Standard of Ur " found in the " Graves of Ur," which latter have been dated c. 3500 B.C., illustrates clearly the civil and military Sumerian costume of this remote period. The " Standard " has a background of a dark pitch-like substance and the human figures upon this background are inlaid in white, chiefly white shell, with here and there some details engraved upon them. The Standard forms a part of the collections at the British Museum and Figs. 107 to 110 are taken from it. Fig. 107, that of a man carrying fish, shews a leather kilt

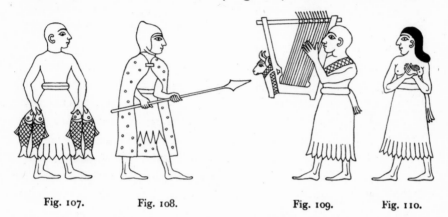

Fig. 107.   Fig. 108.   Fig. 109.   Fig. 110.

with padded belt and the leather at the bottom of kilt has been cut into a sort of fringe of scallops. The head is shaven and the feet are bare. The padded belt so much in evidence on Sumerian costumes is very similar in appearance to that seen on the costumes of Ancient Crete. Fig. 108, that of a spearman, gives us an example of military costume. The kilt here is similar to that of Fig. 107 but it is shorter, and over it the soldier wears a cloak which may be of leather— perhaps the dappled skin of an animal—but, on the other hand, it might be of heavy felted cloth, studded over with small disks of metal. The helmet is probably of leather, though metal helmets were known to the Sumerians even at this very early period. Fig. 109 is that of a harper in a costume practically identical with that of Fig. 107. The

twelve-stringed harp which is carried by this man, though it
is represented in the primitive fashion characteristic of the
Standard of Ur, shews great similarity to an actual harp
which was discovered in the Graves of Ur.   The baldric
worn by the harper is probably for the support of his instrument.   Behind the harper is Fig. 110, a woman singer, in
similar costume.   Her hair, which is not indicated with any
great detail, may be dressed after the manner of that seen
at Fig. 123 (shewn later in this chapter).

Another example of Sumerian costume is seen at Fig. 111.
The original is now in the Louvre and is executed in low
relief.   The date is *c.* 2900 B.C.   This relief represents Ur-
Nina " Patesi " or Ruler of the city of Lagash.   He is
carrying a mason's basket on his head, symbolizing his
founding of a temple.   The Sumerian kilt here has the full
sheep's fleece upon it and this is indicated in a highly
conventional manner which suggests flounces, but is merely
meant to represent a natural sheepskin, perhaps combed and

Fig. 111.

Fig. 112.

trimmed to give this flounced effect. The customary shaven head and unshod feet are seen as is usual at this period.

Fig. 112 is said by some authorities to be Dudu, Prime Minister to Ur-Nina, while others identify it as Lidda, daughter of the Patesi. In any case the costume is practically identical with that of Fig. 111 save that here is an example of the wrap-round kilt being of sufficient length of material to enable a portion to be drawn up under the belt at the back and thrown forwards over the left shoulder forming a little cape on that side. The head here is covered with hair, or it may be a wig. The original relief in the Louvre is somewhat damaged and imperfect, but there is a suggestion that the coiffure may be arranged in similar fashion to that of Fig. 123 (shewn later in this chapter). Figs. 111 and 112 with their extraordinarily primitive air are irresistibly suggestive of Adam and Eve in their " coats of skins."

Two further examples of Sumerian dress are given at Figs. 113 and 114. Fig. 113 is from a limestone relief found

Fig. 113.

Fig. 114.

at Ur which shews the costume of a charioteer holding the reins in his hand. The hair is long, or it may be that the head is covered by a wig similar to those seen in Ancient Egypt. The kilt here is very short, and probably has its opening at the centre front which is covered with a separate hanging piece which conceals the opening; this example may be a more ancient type of kilt than Figs. 107 to 110. The last example of this style of costume is Fig. 114, from the well-known " Stele of the Vultures," now in the Louvre. The date is *c*. 2800 B.C. It represents Eannatum, King or Chief of Sipourla, advancing on the foe at the head of his phalanx of warriors. He wears an ankle-length sheepskin kilt and over it a large shawl or cloak of skin of a finer texture. His helmet is of ancient Sumerian design and almost identical in shape with that seen on the Standard of Ur, Fig. 108, except that here there is a chignon of hair added at the back and a fillet to keep the chignon in place.

We have an actual helmet found in the Graves of Ur known as the Golden Helmet of Mes-Kalam-Dug, dating *c*. 3000 B.C. This specimen differs in shape from that of Eannatum, as it is designed to exactly reproduce an elaborately dressed head of hair and therefore has no peak at the top, but is the shape of the crown of the human head; it resembles the woman's coiffure shewn at Fig. 121. The helmet of Eannatum has no detail except the chignon and fillet. Eannatum holds in his left hand a spear and in his right a weapon which has the appearance of a boomerang. Fig. 115 seems to be the figure of a foreigner (the original is now in the Louvre); it dates *c*. 3000 B.C. The costume consists of a kilt, but in this case it may be of woven material with a fringe. The feathers on the head-dress can be compared with those worn by Asiatic chieftains as represented

by the ancient Egyptians (*see* Fig. 73*c*).   The object held in
the left hand is an oar.   No doubt the change of style which
will be seen in the following examples had some transitional
stages, but if so we have very little evidence to go upon.
There is one statuette in the round
of a Sumerian ruler, dating early
third millenium B.C. which shews a
drapery reaching up to the right
armpit and over the left shoulder
after the manner seen on Fig. 117*a*,
118 and 119, but the material appears still to be sheepskin with the
fleece shaved off and with a scal-
loped or fleecy border at the bottom.
All evidence goes to show, however,
that the change of style seen in the
dress of Gudea of Lagash (Fig. 117*a*)

Fig. 115.

compared with that of Ur-Nina of Lagash (Fig. 111) was
brought about by outside influences and the introduction
of woven materials which now superseded the old sheepskin
dresses.

It has been already stated in this chapter that though the
Sumerians were very primitive in their costume, they were
more advanced in other arts, notably in the art of metal-
working.   The Golden Helmet of Mes-Kalam-Dug, to which
reference has already been made, is one example of Sumerian
skill in this art, but another treasure also found in the Graves
of Ur is an even more striking specimen of highly developed
skill in design and execution.   This is the " Golden Crown of
Queen Shubad," which is exhibited on a beautifully modelled
reconstruction of the head in the British Museum.   The
coiffure is a massive black wig, thick as those worn in

Ancient Egypt.   If it were otherwise the crown would be too large for the head.   The design of this wonderful crown, besides exhibiting a mastery of the precious metals, shews an exquisite appreciation of the beauties of leaf and flower. Raised high above the diadem is an ornament in thin beaten gold.   Long-pointed rays like those of a star rise some inches above the head, and at the tip of each ray hangs a rosette-shaped flower with a jewel in its heart.   Then round the head itself the design consists of rows of hanging leaves executed with great truth to nature.   The first row is of willow leaves, narrow and elegant, the next row is of beech leaves, beautifully veined and with a crystal jewel, like a dewdrop, at the tip of each leaf.   Below the leaves there hangs a row of thin golden rings which overlap one another in their profusion.   Altogether the crown is something to wonder at and admire.   With it were worn a massive series of necklaces and large and elaborate ear-rings.   All these were found buried with the queen in her sepulchre.   The court ladies who shared her grave wore, some golden and others silver, hair-ribbons.   These elaborate ornaments seem to have died out before the next period or style in costume ; the hair of the later centuries being kept in place then by a simple padded fillet, or a flat gold ornament across the front of the head, pierced and tied with ribbons at the back (*see* Figs. 120 and 123), or again we see at Fig. 121 a simple flat fillet and at Fig. 122*a* *b* and *c* a fillet over a veil or net.

CHAPTER X

BABYLONIAN STYLE IN COSTUME

IT has been already explained that the period of Babylonian rule in Mesopotamia is, broadly speaking, from about 2000 B.C. ; but the change of style in costume, a style which seems to have been introduced from the north and possibly the east, took place earlier.

Fig. 116 is from the " Stele of Naram-Sin," *c.* 2500 B.C. and now in the Louvre. Naram-Sin was one of the successors of the Semitic conqueror, Sargon, who has been identified

Fig. 116.

with Nimrod of the Old Testament (who made himself King of Sumer and Agade, *c.* 2600 B.C.). The stele was found at Susa, where it had been taken in later years as war booty by the King of Elam. In this piece of sculpture there is a noticeable advance in the art of representation, when, for example, we compare it with the Standard of Ur. Naram-Sin is in military dress. He is not clothed in skins, but in a fringed wrap-round kilt of woven stuff with a small shawl, also woven, thrown over his left shoulder and knotted corner-wise over the right hip. His helmet is high and is decorated with two horns, also it is entirely different in its contours from the Sumerian shape such as is worn by Eannatum (Fig. 114). He carries a bow and arrow and in addition a small battle-axe. His feet are encased in beautifully designed sandals of pierced leather. Altogether in Fig. 116 we have an entirely different style of dress, that which was worn by the military leaders of the Sargonid Dynasty.

In Figs. 117*a*, 118 and 119 we have an illustration of civilian state costume from the year *c.* 2370 B.C. till *c.* 2100 B.C. It will be seen that these three personages are all wearing what is practically the same costume and are shewn in front view (Fig. 117*a*), left-side view (Fig. 118) and right-side view (Fig. 119). Fig. 117*a* is that of Gudea the Sumerian ruler or Patesi of Lagash, *c.* 2370 B.C. (the original is now in the Louvre). Fig. 117*a* shews in its execution the very great advance in the art of representation which took place between this period, *c.* 2370 B.C., and the period of Ur-Nina, who was Patesi of Lagash, *c.* 2900 B.C. There is no head on this original statue of Gudea, in the Louvre, but in the drawing (Fig. 117*a*) the head has been restored from a contemporary portrait-head of Gudea, also in the Louvre. Fig. 117*b*, *c* and *d* : This drapery is from the figure of the King Gudea,

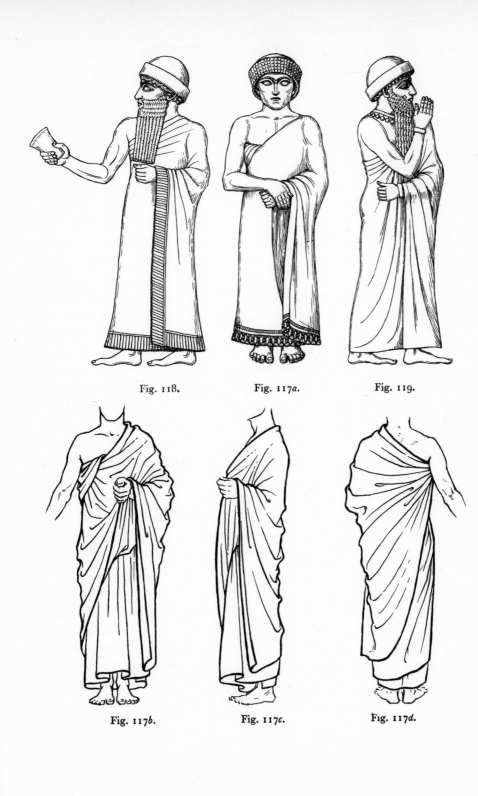

Fig. 118. Fig. 117a. Fig. 119.

Fig. 117b. Fig. 117c. Fig. 117d.

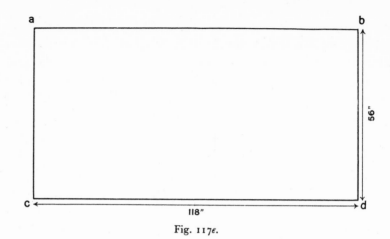

Fig. 117*e*.

2500 B.C. (*see* British Museum). To drape : place the corner *b* of Fig. 117*e* under left armpit, and draw the edge *b–a* round the back of shoulders under the right armpit, across the front of chest, and round the back again, and under the right armpit once more ; then throw the edge *b–a* upwards across the chest and over the left shoulder ; the corner *a* will then hang down the back.   Take this corner *a* and tuck it in at the right side of breast, as shown in illustration (Fig. 117*b*). It should be noted that, unless the left hand is raised, the left arm and hand are entirely covered by this drapery, the right arm only being left free for movement.   This dignified drapery presents points of similarity to the Roman toga of a much later period.   The turban-like head-dress worn by the Patesi is practically identical with that of Figs. 118 and 119, but his face is clean shaven, whereas the other two figures are bearded.   Gudea has the typical Sumerian face, which is seen in front view and profile as well at Figs. 122*a* and *c*. The method of adjusting the drapery is explained in detail at Figs. 117*b*, *c* and *d*.   These latter drawings being made

from actual drapery on a lay figure were worked out from
a statuette of Gudea in the British Museum collection, of a
similar type to the Louvre example 117*a*.   Figs. 118 and
119 are two additional examples of the draped shawl similar
in style to that of Gudea and shewing a left and right view of
the drapery.   Fig. 118 is that of Ur-Nammu, first king of the
3rd Dynasty of Ur, *c.* 2300 B.C.   In Fig. 119 we have a
representation of the celebrated lawgiver, King Hammurabi,
who made Babylon his capital in 1940 B.C. and who is said to
have been a contemporary of Abraham.   It will be seen that
the fashion of shaving the beard has now died out, except
for the upper lip, the faces are fully bearded at both Figs.
118 and 119.   (It is interesting to note that a shawl-drapery
not dissimilar to the Babylonian is worn at the present time
in certain parts of Africa, noticeably in the dress of the women
of Mendiland and Zanzibar.)

As is usually the case in Asiatic regions, the representation
of men's dress is much more frequent than that of women.
However, in Fig. 120 we have a statuette of a seated woman
(from the Louvre) which dates about the middle of the
third millenium B.C. anterior to the period of Gudea.   This

Fig. 120.

costume appears to be a tunic, and it is made of that tufted material called by the Greeks " Kaunakes," which imitated the effect of the earlier sheepskin costumes in weaving. This must have been done either by sewing hanks of wool on to a woven background or by weaving with loops after the manner of Turkish towelling.   The hair of Fig. 120 is worn in simple natural style and kept in place by a padded fillet. The lady holds in her hand what appears to be a small bottle, or leather pouch in the form of a bottle. In Fig. 121, which dates from the first half of the third millenium B.C., we have a portrait head which shews, in addition, another example of the Kaunakes material in the costume. The head is Sumerian in style and was found at Djoka (ancient Oumma). It is now in the Louvre. The hairdressing here is worthy of note because it almost exactly reproduces that which has already been described as being used for a decoration of the Golden Helmet of Mes-Kalam-Dug, one of the treasures of the Graves of Ur (see p. 112). It would seem as if the men and women of this period used, on occasion, the same style in hairdressing. Compare also Fig. 121 with the helmet of Eannatum (Fig. 114).

Fig. 122a, b and c are from a statuette of the middle of the third millenium B.C.   It was discovered at Lagash and is now in the Louvre. This delightful little figure is in an excellent state of preservation, save that, unfortunately, the lower part is missing. The characteristic Sumerian face is here well portrayed with its heavy eyebrows, large round eyes and rather broad full cheeks. The type is said to resemble one which is still found among some of the inhabitants of India in our own day. (Compare the face of Fig. 122a with that of Gudea, Fig. 117a.) The hair of Fig. 122a is turned up into a chignon and covered with a smoothly

Fig. 122*a*.

Fig. 121.

Fig. 122*b*.

Fig. 122*c*.

E

Fig. 122*d*.

9

E

Fig. 122*e*.

E

Fig. 122*f*.

fitting veil or net held in place by a broad fillet. The " dog-collar " necklace is also typical of the women's dress of this period. This statuette shews another example of a draped shawl forming a complete costume as it does in Figs. 117, 118 and 119 (Gudea, Ur-Nammu and Hammurabi). The method of draping Fig. 122 is, however, entirely different from that used for the male costumes, and in effect it seems, in its front view, more symmetrical as both shoulders are covered.

The shape of the scarf or shawl here is almost that of a

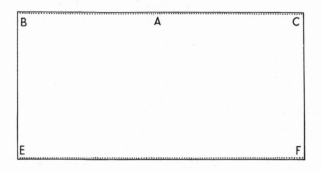

Fig. 122g.

double square (*see* Fig. 122g) and the width is from chest to feet of the wearer. To drape it, take the centre (A) of the top or upper edge (BAC) and place it against the centre of chest (*see* Fig. 122d). Then pass both sides of BAC under each armpit. Cross the two ends of the drapery over at the back. The left side should be underneath and the right side on top. Then draw the two corners (B and C) over the shoulders so that they fall down in front as shewn in the diagrams Figs. 122d, e and f. The corner (E) from the bottom edge of the drapery is seen at the right side of the costume while the corner (F) is hidden underneath. This example is somewhat similar in effect to draperies seen in Ancient Egypt. Compare it, for example, with Figs. 96 and 98a.

In Figs. 123 and 124 we have two costumes from a seal-impression, dating middle of the third millenium B.C. or

Fig. 123.   Fig. 124.

rather later. The subject of this relief is that of the intro-duction of a woman worshipper to a seated goddess (the seated goddess is not here shewn) by a lesser assistant deity.

The woman worshipper (Fig. 123) is clothed in a fringed drapery which distinctly resembles those worn by Figs. 117a, 118 and 119, except that one end of the shawl worn by Fig. 123 is drawn *over* the right arm, not *under* it as it is in the case of the three male costumes. The method of head adornment shews none of that elaboration which has been described as characterizing that of Queen Shubad of the Graves of Ur (*see* p. 114), where also this seal was discovered, but on the other hand it is interesting to note that the tied-up queue of

hair at the back survives as a manner of hairdressing as late
as sixth century B.C., where it can be found, on the heads of
both men and women, both in Greek sculpture and vase
painting. The goddess (Fig. 124) wears a fleecy Kaunakes
costume. It takes the form of a wrap-round skirt with one
end of sufficient length to be drawn up at the back, passed
across and under the right armpit, and then thrown backwards to cover the left shoulder. Fig. 124 wears the horned
mitre or " Cap of Power " which is the sign of divinity ;
indeed this costume is identical with that of the male gods
of this era. Both Figs. 123 and 124 wear the heavy " dog-
collar " necklace so popular at this period and until the
seventh century B.C. where it is seen in wear on Queen
Ashur-Sharrat, wife of Ashur-bani-pal (see Plate VII).

Fig. 125a to f shews the costume of an Elamite lady,
dating c. 2000 B.C. The original, an ivory statuette, is now
in the Louvre. The head and much of the left arm are
missing (the latter has been restored in the drawing at
Fig. 125a). The costumes of the Land of Elam (lying as it
did on the Indian side of the Persian Gulf) shew, in this
and in other examples, a distinct affinity with the dress of
India. Compare Fig. 125a to f with the drawings of a modern
Indian sari at Figs. 95a to d, p. 91. The drapery of Fig. 125
consists of a long shawl or scarf which completely covers the
whole person. It measures about 155 inches by 55 inches.
One end is rectangular but the other seems to be rounded off
into a semicircle (see diagram Fig. 125 f).

Fig. 125c, d and e are drawn from a reconstruction
draped upon an artist's lay figure. The method of draping
is as follows: Let the corner A (Fig. 125f) hang down over
the right shoulder and chest as far as the knee. Pass the
upper edge of the garment backwards over the right shoulder

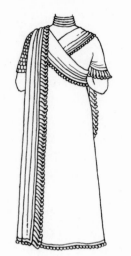

Fig. 125a.   Fig. 125b.

Fig. 125c.   Fig. 125d.   Fig. 125e.

and on towards the left armpit, under the left armpit and loosely across the chest, under the right armpit, then upwards across the back to the top of the left shoulder. Now gather up a little of the slack edge running across the chest and pin the front of drapery to back of same on the top of the left shoulder, as seen in diagrams 125c and d. The rectangular corner A hangs down in front as far as the knee, while the semicircle joining the edge AC at C forms the corner C which is seen at the back, left side, where it touches the ground. The costume shews a short sleeve in another material, seemingly of embossed stuff, which covers the upper part of the left arm. This evidently belongs to a garment underneath the drapery. Possibly this may be a long tunic, but on the other hand it very much suggests the brassière or bust-bodice (the " choli ") worn to-day by many Indian women under their saris.

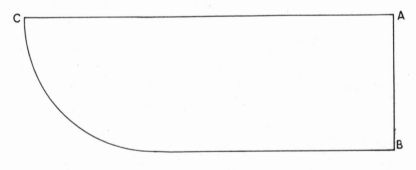

Fig. 125f.

Figs. 126 and 127 are two Elamite costumes from a bas-relief found at Susa and now in the Louvre. These two examples are of a later age than Fig. 125a and b and are dated c. 1000 B.C.–540 B.C., belonging to the Assyrio-Elamite period. Fig. 126, who is evidently an attendant holding a

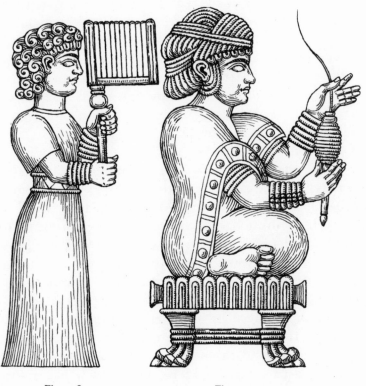

Fig. 126.   Fig. 127.

fan or possibly a fly-whisk, is clad in a simple tunic with belt,
such as is seen on Assyrian women of this period. Her hair
is a short coiffure of elaborate curls. Fig. 127, seated and
holding a spindle on which the thread is wound, seems to be
clad in a drapery not unlike that of Fig. 125, though it is not
very clearly indicated. The head, however, shews a most
elaborate arrangement of twisted coils, and for that reason
the representation is of great interest. From the period
2000 B.C. it is permissible to use the term " Babylonian " in

speaking not only of the costume but of the dynasty; but it will be remembered that the draped style which has been described as Babylonian costume was worn by rulers of previous eras, namely, Sumerian, Accadian and Elamite. At Fig. 119 was illustrated an early Babylonian king wearing the dress seen also on the Sumerian rulers, Gudea and Ur-Nammu; Fig. 119 being a representation of the great king and lawgiver, Hammurabi, c. 2000 B.C. of the 1st Dynasty of Babylon.

Fig. 128a and b shews the costume of a late Babylonian monarch, Marduk-Nadin-Akhe, c. 1050 B.C., from a stele in basalt now in the British Museum. Here, it will be seen, the style of dress has completely changed from that of the early Babylonian rulers. In fact, Marduk-Nadin-Akhe is clothed in a style of dress which we see on the kings of Assyria as late as the ninth century B.C. (compare Fig. 128a with Fig. 129). Fig. 128a shews the general effect of the costume apart from its ornament, while Fig. 128b gives the shape and decorations of the garments worn, which are so similar in style to those of the Assyrian kings. Firstly, the head-dress or tiara should be noted, as it has a surprising history of survival. We see it, for example, with the addition of six horns at Fig. 153d as an Assyrian example, and it survives also through the ancient Persian era. Perhaps the most strange fact of all is that, shorn of its decorations, we can see it to-day used as a head-dress by the clergy of the Eastern Orthodox Christian Church. The short-sleeved, ankle-length tunic which covers most of the king's person is surmounted by a small fringed shawl wrapped round the hips and kept in place by a broad waist-belt. The feet are shod, not in sandals but in shoes. There is a double baldric seen crossed over on the breast which probably supports at

Fig. 128a.

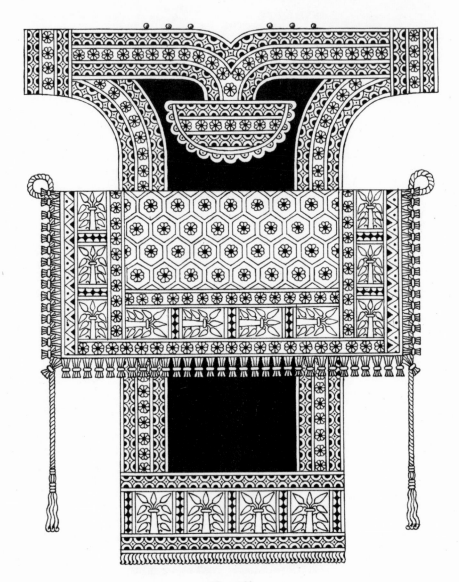

Fig. 128b.

the back a weapon and perhaps a quiver for the arrows which Marduk-Nadin-Akhe is carrying. The shaping of tunic and shawl are seen at Fig. 128*b* as also the elaborate decoration, which latter was probably executed in tapestry-darning by similar methods to those used on the ancient Egyptian tunics which are still preserved to us in various museum collections. As will be seen, the detail of the ornament is almost entirely geometric save that round the edges of the shawl and at the bottom of the tunic we find that well-known Mesopotamian symbol, the " Tree of Life " or " Sacred Tree," which can be observed in later centuries as a motif in the decorative art of the Assyrian Empire. As will be seen in Chapter XI, the costume of this Babylonian king, Marduk-Nadin-Akhe, at Fig. 128, remains as a style for the Assyrian kings throughout the period of their domination.

CHAPTER XI

ASSYRIAN STYLE IN COSTUME

THE Assyrian Empire began its career of conquest *c.* 1100 B.C. and the characteristic costume seems to have reached its full development by that date, also the style survived practically unchanged until the overthrow of the Assyrians by the Medes and Persians. We are fortunate in having access to the rich results of the many explorations in Assyria which began towards the middle of the nineteenth century. In particular there exist, in splendid preservation, very numerous examples of sculpture in low relief, where we see the life of this great empire laid bare in the utmost detail. As we might expect of a race of warriors, battle scenes predominate in the representations—chiefly we have great rulers and their soldiers in the panoply of war. Then also we have the tributaries and captives and here again it is abundantly evident that the Assyrian artists were keenly interested in the costumes of other nations, and took pains to represent them with exactitude. Our knowledge of women's costume in Assyria is most frequently gained from the dress of women captives, but, as is usual in the East, much more care and enthusiasm is taken in the representation of the dress of men. Besides the costume of the armies, there are preserved to us sculptures in relief shewing the costume of musicians, huntsmen, fishermen and so forth. Most frequently represented of all Assyrian costumes is the dress of the great king. We see these monarchs in battle-dress, hunting-dress and in stately ceremonial dress throughout the Assyrian era. These royal costumes, moreover, are generally lavishly ornamented. Besides the heavy jewellery which was worn, the dresses are as a rule almost entirely covered with the richest decoration. This decoration, however, shews little variety, and the patterns which are seen on the costume of that late Babylonian monarch, Marduk-Nadin-Akhe (Fig. 128*b*) are the inspiration of the ornament of the succeeding era. The royal costumes almost invariably consist of a full-length tunic and frequently over that is draped a shawl or shawls.

Fig. 129 is one of the many representations of the great

Fig. 129.

Assyrian, King Ashur-nasir-pal, ninth century B.C.   The differences between Figs. 128 and 129 are chiefly in the head-dress and footwear.   Instead of the tiara seen at Fig. 128, Fig. 129 has a cap of soft material, probably felt, which, in spite of the conical projection at the top, is strikingly similar to the modern " fez " or " tarbush " now worn in South-Western Asia and North Africa.   Next we notice that the belt of the Assyrian king is much wider than that of his Babylonian predecessor ;   last of all, while Marduk-Nadin-Akhe is wearing shoes, Ashur-nasir-pal has sandals on his feet.   At Fig. 129 the small shawl does not go completely round the hips and is seen only at the back, not wrapped right round, and it would therefore measure only about 20 inches square.   A second type of Assyrian royal costume has as its foundation the full-length tunic, but over this there is draped a large square shawl which covers the whole form from waist to bottom of tunic, while a smaller shawl drapes the upper part of the body ;   this latter shawl is of semicircular shape.   An excellent illustration of this type of Assyrian royal dress is seen in a statuette of the same monarch, Ashur-nasir-pal, as at Fig. 129.   This is Fig. 130 now in the British Museum.   The drawing (Fig. 130) shews this statuette in front view.   Here the king is bare-headed.   He holds a mace in his left hand and a curved toothed weapon in his right.   This type of royal costume—a long tunic draped with shawls—was worn for at least two hundred years ; as well as the examples given of the ninth century B.C., we see it on a relief of the Assyrian king, Esarhaddon, seventh century B.C.—the said relief forming part of the collection at the Berlin Museum.   The method of arranging the shawl draperies is indicated after a rather conventionalized and primitive fashion by the Assyrian artists.   It is, therefore,

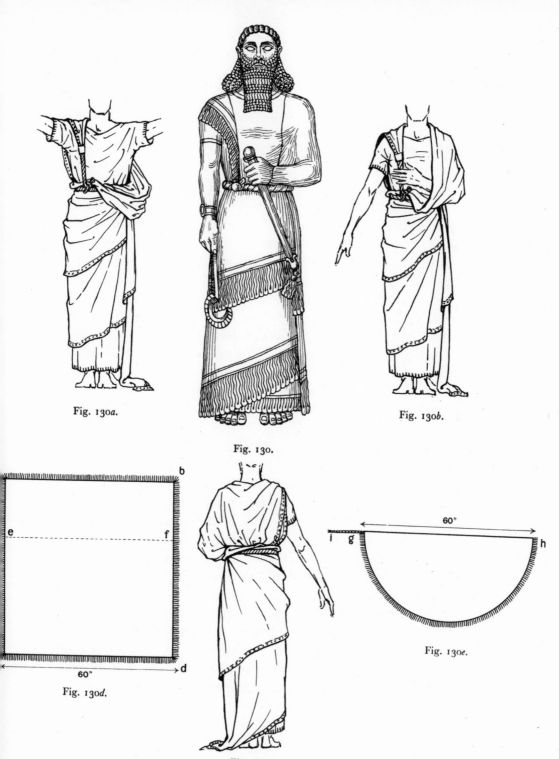

Fig. 130a.

Fig. 130.

Fig. 130b.

Fig. 130d.

Fig. 130c.

Fig. 130e.

necessary to explain the construction by the illustrations at Fig. 130*a*, *b*, *c* and *d*, where the shape of the two shawls used and the method of arranging them is shewn—the latter upon an artist's lay figure. To achieve the effect proceed as follows : Take the square shawl (Fig. 130*d*) and fold outwards about 20 inches as at *e–f*. Tie a waist-cord on the tunic and tuck the corner *f* deeply into it at the left side of waist, then draw tightly round the figure in front and round again across the back of waist till the left side is reached again. Now double about 6 inches of the shawl inwards, and tuck in again into waist-cord. Then take the semicircular shawl (Fig. 130*e*) and attach the cord *i–g* to the waist-cord. Throw this shawl backwards over the right shoulder and arrange it as a sling over the left arm (*see* drawing 130*b*). The corner of this shawl shews in front about 8 inches below the waist towards the left. Tie a second waist-cord tightly over all to keep the upper shawl in position.

Still another representation of King Ashur-nasir-pal gives a variant of the tunic over-draped with shawl. This is seen at Plate VI (2) and in the explanatory drawings at Fig. 131*a* to *c*. Plate VI (2) is a representation of the king from an enamelled tile decoration. His head-dress here shews the pendant lappets at the back, which are similar to those pendant bands (called " *infulae* " by the mediaeval Christian church of the West) which are seen hanging down at the back of a bishop's mitre. To drape the shawl as seen at Plate VI (2) proceed as follows (the shawl's dimensions are given at Fig. 131*a*) : Take the garment and fold over on the line *e–f* so that *e*, *f*, *a*, *b* hangs down outside ; then take the cord *e–g*, as illustrated, and hold *g* at right side of waist in front (*see* Fig. 131*b*), throwing the remainder of the shawl backwards

PLATE V

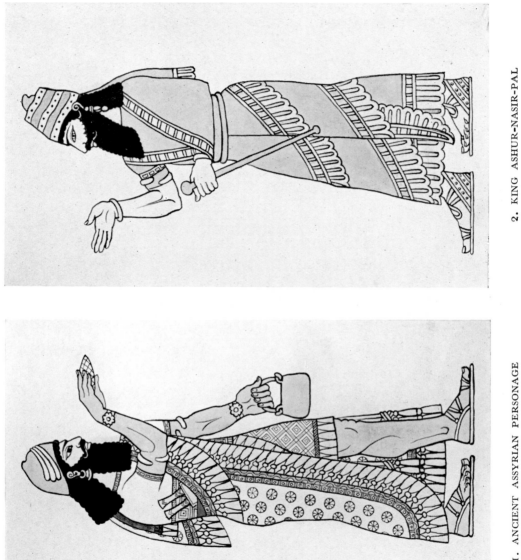

PLATE VII

QUEEN ASHUR-SHARRAT

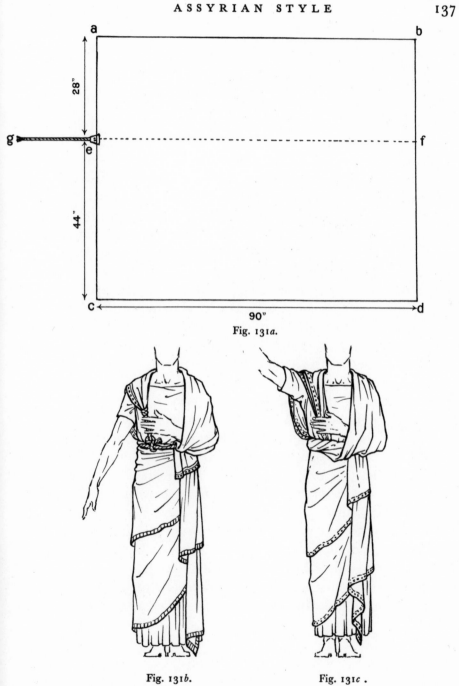

Fig. 131a.

Fig. 131b.   Fig. 131c.

over the right shoulder. Draw the edge *e–f* round the back of neck and form a sling over the left arm as shewn. To complete the draping, continue to pass the edge *e–f* round the waist towards the right, passing under the right arm at waist level, then on round the back and left side, until it reaches about 6 inches in front of left side of waist ; now fold the remainder of drapery underneath, as shewn in the drawings, and tie a cord round waist to keep all firmly in position ; knot the end of the cord *e–g* to this waist-cord. Fig. 130*c* shews the back view and Fig. 130*d* shews the drapery thrown off the left shoulder to give freedom to both arms (Fig. 131*b* and *c* giving freedom to the right arm only). If the cord *e–g* is pulled down so that *e* touches the waist, then both shoulders will be covered by the drapery. Fig. 131*b* is one method of arranging the shawl as seen at Plate VI (2), but the effect can also be achieved without the added waist-cord or small attached cord, *e–g*. To drape as at Fig. 131*c*, take the same shawl and make a somewhat deeper fold-over. The point *e* should be pinned or knotted to the waist-cord of tunic. Then, while arranging the remainder of the drapery after previous method, keep rolling it at the waist while it is being adjusted. When worn thus, with a roll of itself, the drapery will remain in position, but it is not quite so secure as when confined with an added waist-cord. On the whole, this drapery with the large shawl or shawls must have been reserved for occasions of ceremony where movement was slow and dignified. On the other hand, the short shawl wrapped round the hips would not impede the limbs to any extent, as indeed it was worn in battle. Plate VI (1) (from the British Museum) is described as " a mythological figure in attendance upon King Ashur-nasir-pal " (ninth century B.C.). In this costume we have a knee-length

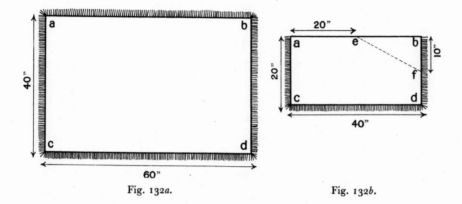

Fig. 132a.   Fig. 132b.

tunic, with a small wrap-round shawl (as at Fig. 128a and
Fig. 128a also shews the wide belt seen at Plate VI (1)).
Over the tunic and small shawl is thrown a larger shawl.

The combination of garments here seen may be said to
constitute a third style when compared with the first style
seen at Fig. 129 and the second at Fig. 130a and Plate VI (2),
but this third type is nothing like so frequently represented
as the former two. The method of arranging the two shawls
at Plate VI (1) is easily explained by reference to the drawings
at Fig. 132a and b where the shape and dimensions are
given. To drape, proceed as follows : Take the small
shawl (Fig. 132b) and place the corner a on the right hip,
pass the edge a–b across the front towards the left and round
the waist. The triangle b, e, f, can be tucked into a waist-
cord tied over the tunic ; then the wide belt (probably of
leather) is put on and to keep it in position it is held by a
narrow over-belt, into which latter, it will be seen, two
daggers are thrust (compare with the belt of Fig. 129).
Lastly, the large shawl (Fig. 132a) has the corner b tucked
into the narrow belt at left side of waist and the edge a–b

passed round the back towards the right side of waist, upwards and across the chest, and hangs down at the back over the left shoulder. In the original the figure seen at Plate VI (1) is winged, but here the wings have been omitted. It will be seen that the head-dress of this personage is decorated with horns as is that at Fig. 124, these being the symbol of divinity and the head-dress, therefore, known as the Cap of Power. The feet at Plate VI (1) are in sandals, similar to those seen at Fig. 129 and Plate VI (2). Fig. 133*a* and *b* are described as " two heavily armed warriors in mail, before a city." They are from Nimroud and of the period of Ashur-nasir-pal. It will be seen that *a* carries a shield and dagger while *b* is armed with a bow and sword, also *a* is bare-footed while *b* has sandals. The conical helmets are characteristic and with their pendant curtains of mail form a very complete protection for the head. The mail itself most probably consists of small metal plates sewn on to a foundation of leather or stoutly woven cloth.

Fig. 134 shews a lightly armed soldier of the same period, also from Nimroud. He is clad in a richly patterned shawl, which forms a wrap-round kilt ; he also wears the wide Assyrian belt with the narrow over-belt to hold the former in place. His double baldric supports a quiver full of arrows and a sword or dagger. In addition to his bow he holds a small mace. His feet are bare and we note that his helmet is identical in shape with those of the two heavily armed warriors at Fig. 133*a* and *b*, though there is no pendant curtain of mail covering the neck and chin in this case.

Fig. 135—a musician playing a stringed instrument from the court of King Ashur-nasir-pal, again from Nimroud—is an example of a dignified civilian dress of the period. Over his long tunic, which is without decoration except for a

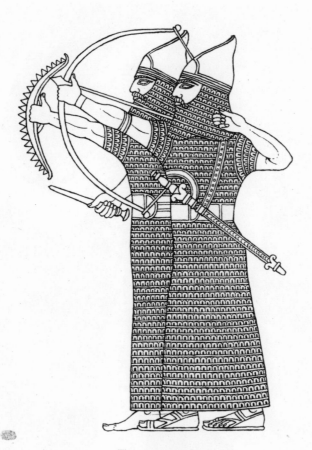

Figs. 133*a*, 133 *b*.

fringe at the bottom, he wears, by way of a belt, a fringed
band, which would be about 12 inches wider than the
waist and so could be well wrapped over and tucked in to
keep it in position, and this is made clear in the drawing.
The handsome fringed baldric is, of course, needed to support
the harp.

Fig. 134.

Fig. 135.

Figs. 136 and 137 are the costumes of two captive women which are also of the period of Ashur-nasir-pal. These do not call for special remark, save perhaps that it should be noted that the belt of Fig. 136 is of that padded type seen in early Sumerian costume (compare here with Figs. 107 to 112) and which is also a feature in the dress of the far-distant Mediterranean island of Crete from the second millenium B.C. Fig. 137 shews the long tunic with fringed hem so

universally worn at this period. The method of representation
is rather primitive, and the shawl which covers the head and
drapes the figure would in reality be full of folds not here
shewn.

Fig. 138 represents the costume of a third woman, a
captive of the period of King Sennacherib (eighth and seventh
centuries B.C.). Over her long plain tunic this woman wears
a shawl which is fringed at either end and measures about
50 inches by 80 inches. To drape this shawl, place one
corner under the left armpit and draw it across the back
under the right armpit, wrapping it once round the body ;
draw it then across the back and over the right shoulder.
A corner of the fringed end will hang down in front of the
right shoulder.

Fig. 139 is from the head of an ivory statuette (this head
being discovered at Nimroud) and the date is ninth to eighth
centuries B.C. The jewelled close-fitting cap and the heavy
jewelled necklace indicate that the wearer was clothed with
great luxury. Later examples of Assyrian costume than those
already described (which it will be remembered are chiefly
associated with the period of Ashur-nasir-pal, ninth century
B.C.) may be best represented by the costume of the reign of
that greatest of late Assyrian monarchs, King Ashur-bani-pal.
As has been already stated, no great change is discernible
between the costumes of the earlier and later Assyrian
epochs. What differences there are seem in part to be due
to the introduction of certain details from the costume of
foreigners. For example, Fig. 140 shews a man in hunting
dress and Figs. 141 and 142 two military costumes. These
three costumes can be compared with that of a foreigner
(Fig. 143) especially in the matter of footwear, where it
would certainly seem as if the earlier Assyrian sandal was

Fig. 136.

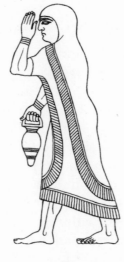

Fig. 137.

Fig. 138.

Fig. 140.

Fig. 139.

superseded by high laced boots from some outside source, such as may be seen here at Fig. 143. Again, the helmets at Figs. 141 and 142 differ from the conical type seen at Figs. 133 and 134. Indeed Fig. 141 has a helmet which is not unlike a certain type worn by the warriors of Ancient Greece in a later age. But it must be remembered that the typical conical Assyrian helmet was not superseded by these foreign influences. The mounted horseman, seen at Fig. 152, for example, though of the late period, still wears the conical helmet also worn two centuries earlier. Fig. 143 itself, where the high boots are so much in evidence, is a foreigner from a relief at Nineveh. The careful delineation of the animal's skin worn by this man as a cloak is a further example of the pains which the Assyrian artists took to represent the costume of other nations. Fig. 144a, b and c is again a foreign tributary. The original is seen on the well-known " Black Obelisk of Shalmaneser III," King of Assyria, 859 B.C.–824 B.C. This is one of the men bringing tribute from the King of Khattina. Over his long fringed tunic there is seen a large shawl of the shape indicated at Fig. 144c. The drawing 144b shews it draped upon an artist's lay figure. To arrange this shawl proceed as follows : Take the corner a and throw it backwards over the left shoulder, pass the edge a–b across the chest and under the right armpit ; then draw across the back and throw the corner b over the left shoulder so that it falls down in front as shewn at Fig. 144b—also in Fig. 144a the peaked cap and boots with upturned toes are features to be noted.

Fig. 145a and b. Fig. 145a is a tribute-bearer of uncertain nationality, from a relief at the palace at Khorsabad, built by Sargon II, King of Assyria in 722 B.C.–705 B.C. Fig. 145b is a diagram suggesting the method of cutting the

Fig. 142   Fig. 141.   Fig. 143.

Fig. 144a.   Fig. 144c.   Fig. 144b.

short coat which is part of this costume. It must be remembered that the ancient Assyrians represented costumes as
tight-fitting when a realistic style would have depicted folds.
A similar costume as to head-gear and tunic is seen at Fig.
146, but here the upper garment seems to be open down the
sides and not in front. In fact it can be conceived as being
shaped on the same plan as the " Median Robe of Honour "
as worn by Darius, King of Persia (Plate IX) save that in
the case of Fig. 146 the garment is on a much less voluminous
scale. One authority (A. T. Olmstead) considers it to be
the representation of a Median chief presenting his city's
model to the Assyrian king.

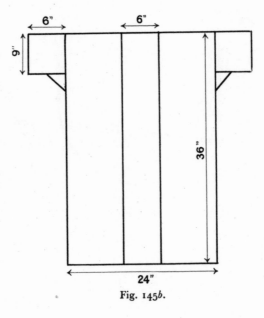

Fig. 145*b*.

Fig. 145a.

Fig. 147.

Fig. 146.

Fig. 147 shews the costume of a bowman, who in addition to his bow also carries a mace. It is from a relief in the British Museum of the period of Tiglath-pileser IV, 747 B.C.–727 B.C. It was found at Nimroud (ancient Calah). Scribes and high officials of the court are seen in similar dress. The very handsome fringed drapery is characteristic. This goes once round the waist, is drawn up from behind, under the left arm, across the chest and is then thrown backwards over the right shoulder.

Fig. 148. This royal costume is from a relief in the British Museum ; it represents the great king, Ashur-bani-pal (668 B.C.–624 B.C.), in hunting dress. Here we have later Assyrian art at its highest. The king has descended from his chariot and is in the act of pouring a libation over the bodies of the lions which he has slain and which, in the original relief, are seen in groups lying on the ground at his feet. When comparing this costume with that of Ashur-nasir-pal (*see* Fig. 129), whose reign, it will be remembered, dates 884 B.C.–860 B.C., we find there is little difference between the two, except that in the later example the tunic is worn alone without a shawl of any kind. In Fig. 148 the detail of the original relief is unfortunately much defaced by time, therefore its silhouette and proportions have been closely followed in the drawing, the ornament is taken from another representation of Ashur-bani-pal. The cutting-out of the tunic would be identical with that of the ancient Babylonian king, Marduk-nadin-akhe (*c.* 1050 B.C.), Fig. 128*b*. As in the earlier example the ornament on Fig. 148 is almost entirely geometric, the exception being that there is a rectangular panel on the breast which has a representation of the winged sun's disk and beneath that a small Tree of Life. The whole design would probably have been executed

Fig. 148.

in wool tapestry-embroidery such as was also the case at
Fig. 128*b*. Plate VII is a representation of Queen Ashur-
Sharrat, the wife of Ashur-bani-pal. She wears a tunic
which is similar to that of the king, but the sleeves in the
queen's are longer and reach halfway down the lower arm ;
her shawl, which is fringed all round, would measure about
50 inches by 130 inches. It is wrapped once round the
lower limbs and so covers the bottom of her tunic ; it is
then wound round the upper part of her body, in similar
fashion to that of the woman at Fig. 138, only going in
the opposite direction. She wears the usual heavy necklace,
ear-rings and bracelets of the period. Her coiffure is extremely
simple. The hair seems to be arranged in precisely similar
fashion to that of her male contemporaries, but it can also
be compared with the coiffure at Fig. 138 (the woman
captive of the period of Sennacherib, eighth and seventh
centuries B.C.). The queen, however, instead of the simple
fillet seen on the captive, wears a jewelled coronet. She
wears shoes on her feet (not sandals) as is also the case in the
representation of her husband (Fig. 148). Two other
examples of women's costume of this late Assyrian period
are seen at Figs. 149*a* and *b* and 150*b*. The two musicians
at Fig. 149*a* and *b* are dressed identically, their costume
consisting as it does of the long, simple, belted tunic worn by
Assyrian women and by their contemporaries in neighbouring
countries. They are taking part in a triumphal procession
which suggests that they are captives, and indeed the looped-
up coiffure also suggests a foreign origin or else the survival
of a very ancient method of hairdressing. Figs. 123 and 124,
dating from the middle of the third millenium B.C., shew the
antiquity of the style, but it also appears as a style for men
on a sculptured head from Nimroud which Layard considers

PLATE VIII

2. ANCIENT ASSYRIAN JEWELLERY AND TASSELS

1. ANCIENT ASSYRIAN DECORATION

PLATE IX

DARIUS, KING OF PERSIA

(See page 162)

may be a captive from Bactria. Then it is frequently found in early Greek art of the sixth century B.C. There is, for example, a bronze head of Zeus from Olympia which shews it, and it is frequently seen as a style for women on Greek vase-paintings as late as the beginning of the fifth century B.C. Altogether, a remarkably widespread and long-continuing fashion in hairdressing reaching out, *in space*, from Bactria in the east, to Greece in the west, and continuing, *in time*, from the middle of the third millenium B.C. until the fifth century B.C.

Fig. 150*b*, a woman captive, of the same period as that of the two musicians, is wearing a costume almost identical with that of Fig. 137 : but the latter has fringes, whereas Fig. 150*b* is without decoration. The child at 150*a* and the fisherman (Fig. 151) shew the short belted tunic worn by men engaged in active pursuits and also by boys at this

Fig. 149*a*. Fig. 149*b*.   Fig. 151.   Fig. 150*a*.   Fig. 150*b*.

period. The last costume illustrating the late Assyrian style
is Fig. 152—a mounted soldier from the Palace of Nineveh
and of the period of Ashur-bani-pal. This shews a fully
developed military dress, having over the usual short tunic
a corselet of mail, also round the hips a wrap-round shawl
which again is kept in place by a wide belt. The lower
limbs are covered after the same manner as those of the

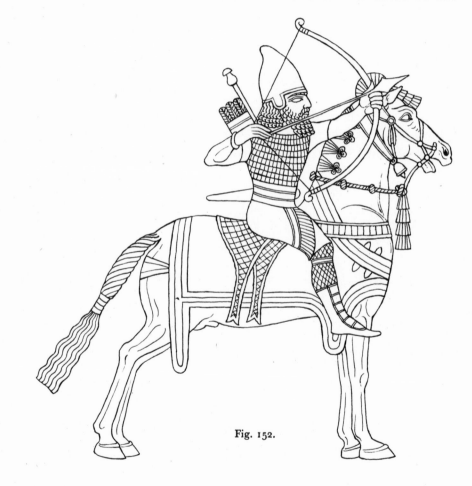

Fig. 152.

spearman at Fig. 141. The tall conical helmet worn in an earlier age by the soldiers of Ashur-nasir-pal (*see* Figs. 133*a* and *b* and 134) is still surviving here in spite of other types having been introduced (*see* Figs. 141 and 142) at this period.

ASSYRIAN ORNAMENT

As has been already said, many of the Assyrian costumes are richly decorated and worn with a lavish display of jewellery. Yet in the detail there is little variety, or even novelty, for we see most of the detail already fixed and standardized on the costume of the Babylonian king, Marduk-nadin-akhe of the eleventh century B.C. (*see* Fig. 128*b*). Assyrian ornament has become known to us through representations on bas-reliefs and on enamelled tiles and bricks where royal personages and their gods are shewn in great magnificence.

Fig. 153*a* to *j* is a collection of Assyrian jewellery and head-dresses giving the effect of these ornaments in relief. The details of Fig. 153 are as follows :

a and *b*—bands such as are used to decorate head-dresses and tunics.

c is a jewelled bandeau for the hair, with a tassel at the back.

e and *i* are ear-rings.

f, *g* and *h* are bracelets.

j is a jewelled tassel.

d is an elaborate example of the horned Cap of Power.

This last specimen differs in shape from the " Cap " seen at Fig. 124, which latter is conical. On the other hand Fig. 153*d* is similar in shape to the tiara at Fig. 128*a*. The horns, it will be remembered, are the symbol of divinity.

The tiara at 153*d* is seen in almost identical form on the heads of two winged genii from the Palace of Susa, imperial Persian art of the sixth to fifth centuries B.C. But the

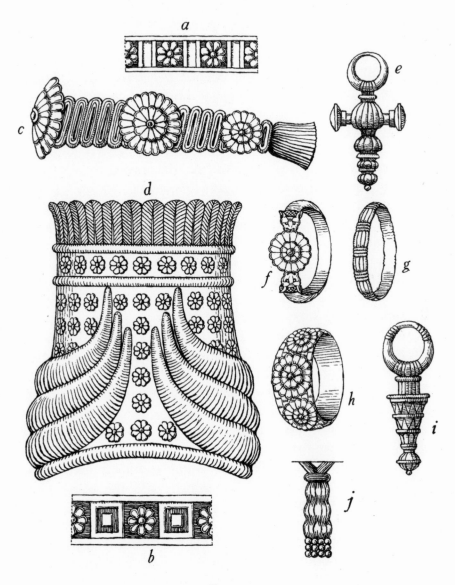

Fig. 153.

survival of this tiara, shorn of its decoration, is remarkable. At the present time it is worn as a head-dress by the clergy of the Eastern Orthodox Church, that is from its presence on the head of a Babylonian king of the eleventh century B.C. until the middle of the twentieth century A.D. There can be few, if any, instances in the history of costume of such long continuance of a style.

Plate VIII (1) gives another set of characteristic Assyrian ornamental details. Here again almost all the motifs are geometric. They are also the decorative details such as are seen embroidered upon garments. Type *a*, the only non-geometric example, is a form of the Sacred Tree or Tree of Life, a form, however, which differs from that seen upon the garments of Fig. 128*a*. A point to be remembered in connection with Plate VIII (1) is the fan-shaped palmette in the centre, which survives in the ornament of Ancient Greece and even of the Roman era—another example of long survival. The types *b*, *c*, *d*, *e*, *f* are repeating patterns from costumes, while *g*, *h*, *i*, *j*, *k*, *l* are borders from the same. Lastly *m* is an elaborate specimen of the rosettes so much used in Assyrian decoration.

Plate VIII (2) (*a* to *o*) shews further details of Assyrian ornament :

a, *b* and *c* are bracelets.

d, *e* and *f* are ear-rings.

g, *h*, *i* and *j* are tassels from costume and from the harness of horses.

k is the " Winged Globe."

This last specimen should be compared with the Egyptian example shewn at Plate IV (2) and also with the Persian illustration shewn at Fig. 157. Each of these three, symbolizing as they do the sun's disk, was held in reverence, but most of all it was adored by the adherents of the Persian religion of Zoroaster as the special symbol of their God, the spirit of all good, Ahura-mazda.

l is a conventional but highly effective rendering of the date-palm which bulked so largely in the food-supply of the Mesopotamian peoples. The fan-shaped head of this tree can be compared with the ornament at Plate VIII (1) *a*, where it would seem nature is still more highly conventionalized, yet the similarity is marked.

m is from the lappet of a king's tiara, where the winged bull, another favourite Assyrian symbol, makes its appearance.

n is a bronze vessel, the ornamental detail of which clearly shews that such vessels first took shape as basket-work and were afterwards copied in bronze. The mytho-logical figure at Plate VI (1) is carrying a vessel of identical shape with *n* (Plate VIII (2)).

o is a geometric ornament of the simplest type. It comes from an engraved sword-handle. Practically all the types of ornament represented on Plate VIII can be seen constantly repeated on the costumes of the great Assyrian bas-reliefs with which the British Museum and the Paris Louvre are sor ichly endowed. The ornament, besides its own intrinsic interest, has a value apart as a fount of inspiration to the ornamental art of later periods and to countries near and also distant as far as the Eastern Mediterranean.

SECTION III

ANCIENT PERSIAN COSTUME

INTRODUCTION

As we know, the short-lived Median Empire preceded that of the Persians, and it was due to the Median conqueror that the fall of the Assyrian Empire took place. However, at the present time our knowledge of the Median Empire is so scanty that the only description of their costume here given is that of their " Robe of Honour," seen in Chapter XII, Plate IX and Figs. 155*a* and 159. It should be said that this garment was adopted by the Persians in whose empire the Medes were treated with respect and consideration.

The costumes which are described in this section date, broadly speaking, from the sixth century B.C. until the seventh century A.D. In style they may be divided into three periods, namely, those of :

(1) The Achaemenid Period from its rise in the sixth century B.C. until the Alexandrine Conquest in the fourth century B.C.

(2) The Seleucid and Arsacid Periods. The former dating from death of Alexander till the second century B.C. and the latter dating from the third century B.C. until the third century A.D.

(3) The Sassanid Period from the third century A.D. until the seventh century A.D.

While Greek influence is seen in both Seleucid and Arsacid styles, in the Sassanid there is a return to Persian inspiration and the Greek fades out so as to be almost imperceptible.

CHAPTER XII

ACHAEMENID, SELEUCID, ARSACID, AND SASSANID PERSIAN COSTUME

THE costume of the Persian Empire differs essentially from that of most other ancient civilizations with which we are familiar. The dress of Ancient Egypt, Sumeria, Babylonia and Assyria, consisting as it does of skirts, shawls and tunics, bears no resemblance to that which is characteristically Persian. In a word, what we see is the contrast between a loose or draped style and that of a costume which consists of a fitted coat and trousers. The home of this trousered costume seems to have been Central Asia, where races of horsemen from time immemorial, clothed themselves in fitted leather garments. On the east of this region we find the wearing of trousers extending into China, while on the west it came with the Scythian tribes into Southern Russia and from thence it crept farther westward still until it reached the Atlantic coast where we are familiar with it in the costume of the ancient Gauls.

Style I

ACHAEMENID COSTUME

While stating the fact that ancient Persian dress consisted essentially of a coat and trousered costume it has to be remembered that the " Median Robe of Honour," to which

reference has been made in the introduction to this Section
(III), formed an important feature in the style. As the Robe
of Honour was the garment most favoured by the Persian
monarch himself—the great king of kings—it is fitting that
it should be first described. This garment is also found in
Ancient Egyptian costume (*see* Plates I (3), II, III (1)), but
the Persian or Median method of wearing it is so different
that at a casual glance the identity of cut or shape is not
apparent. The Medes and Persians arranged it as shewn at
Plate IX and Fig. 155*a*. The method of cutting-out and
draping is explained at Fig. 154*a* and *b*. Compare these with
the explanatory diagrams which accompany Plates I (3), II,
III (1) in the Ancient Egyptian section of this volume.
Plate IX is a representation of Darius, King of Persia,
sixth century B.C. Besides the Robe of Honour the king's
head-dress should be noted. He is seen wearing that characteristic tiara called by the Greeks the " Mitra " (compare
here with Figs. 128*a*, 153*a* and 159). The Robe is cut-out
and draped as follows : Fig. 154*a* is, as will be seen, a doubled
rectangular piece of material, before doubling it would be
twice the height of the wearer. When folded it is sewn up
each side from the bottom, leaving a space of about 20 inches
at the top through which the hands and arms can emerge.
There is a slit left for the head which would be arranged for
while the garment was being woven. When the robe is put
on over the head, a girdle is tightly bound round the waist
and then a portion is pulled up at either side over the girdle
so as to produce the very graceful drapery shewn at Plate
IX, Figs. 154*b* and 155*a*. The result of this draping is to
give great freedom to the arms.

The tight-fitting Persian trousers seem to be indicated
under the robes of both Plate IX and Fig. 155*a*, but the

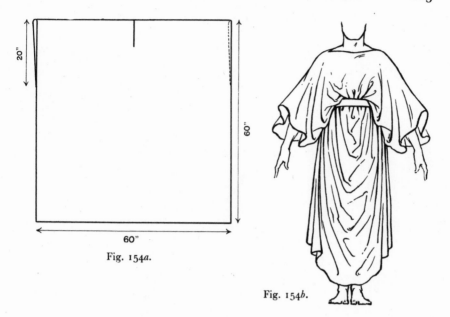

Fig. 154a.

Fig. 154b.

rather elegant shoes are seen with more detail in the second example, which represents a man of the king's bodyguard of archers. It is from the king's palace at Susa. It dates sixth or early fifth century B.C. and is now in the Louvre. This robe is for the most part covered with what must have been embroidery or a tapestry-woven decoration, but there is a plain unornamented band of contrasting colour stretching across the garment ; its width reaching from just underneath the chest to below the hips. The remainder of the robe is decorated with a rosette pattern edged by borders. The detail of this is seen at Fig. 155e. Fig. 155b is a Persian border of the fifth century B.C., now in the museum at Istamboul. Fig. 155d gives the pattern which decorates the immense quiver of Fig. 155a, while 155e shews a fringed

Fig. 155.

and rosette-patterned border from the palace of Xerxes, fifth century B.C.

Before describing the Persian coat and trousers of the Achaemenid Period we may turn to one of the rare representations of women's dress of this time seen at Fig. 156. There is little here which calls for comment. This representation of a Persian lady dates *c.* fifth century B.C. It was found in Asia Minor and is now in the museum at Istamboul. The veil or cloak covers the figure at full length and there seems to be a knee-length tunic over a longer garment underneath. Much of the detail has been obliterated by time, but what is left goes to shew that this lady is not very differently dressed from her Assyrian predecessors. On p. 166 we see at Fig. 157 a representation, in Persian

Fig. 156.

Fig. 157.

art, of the winged globe, which can be compared with the
Egyptian example at Plate IV (2) and the Assyrian type at
Plate VIII (2).   Fig. 157 is a detail from an embroidered
baldachin in bas-relief at the Palace of Xerxes at Persepolis,
fifth century B.C.   It is here a symbol of Ahura-mazda, the
Spirit of All-Good in the Zoroastrian religion.   Fig. 158a, b
and c shews the coat and trousers characteristic of the
Achaemenid Period, and in addition to the tight-fitting coat
or tunic we see an overcoat with ribbons to tie at the
breast.   This is worn, as was frequently the case, after the
manner of a cloak, the arms are not inserted into the sleeves.
A suggested method for cutting the overcoat and trousers is
seen at Fig. 158b and c.   The characteristic Persian head-
dress of the period—the " Kulah "—is worn.   It is a tall
cylindrical cap of felt with, in this case, ribbons pendant at
the back, such as we have seen were worn by the Assyrians
(as for example at Plate VI (2)).   The feet are covered with
the usual plain shoe or boot, which seems to be worn over the
trousers at the ankle.   Figs. 159 and 160 shew the two types
of Persian costume worn simultaneously.   These are men of
the king's bodyguard.   The dress of Fig. 159 is almost
identical in type with that of 155a except that 155a wears a
twisted head-fillet, whereas 159 has the characteristic ribbed
tiara (kidaris).   A costume such as that of Fig. 160 has
already been described at Fig. 158, but in the case of
Fig. 160 no overcoat is worn.   Fig. 161 is again practically

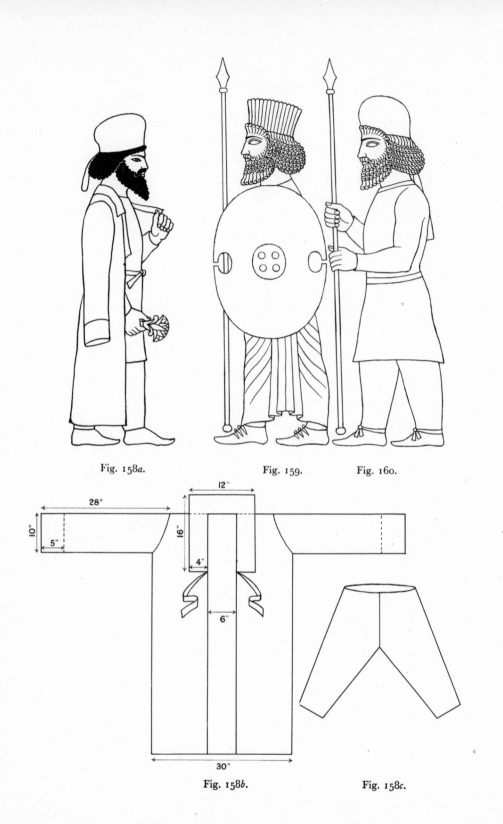

Fig. 158a.

Fig. 159.

Fig. 160.

28"

10"

5"

12"

16"

4"

6"

30"

Fig. 158b.

Fig. 158c.

identical with Fig. 160.   Here is seen a Persian guardsman
leading a procession of tribute-bearing foreigners into the
presence of the great king.   The original of these drawings
is a relief upon the wall of the Great Staircase of the Palace
of Xerxes at Persepolis, fifth century B.C.   Fig. 162 is a
Scythian, Fig. 163, an Indian ; Fig. 164, a Bactrian ; Fig.
165, an Armenian and Fig. 166, an Anatolian.   Three of
these costumes are of the trousered Persian type ; that of the
Indian a complete contrast, while the Anatolian more nearly
approaches the costume of Fig. 167a which is also a tribute-
bearer of the fifth century B.C. from Persepolis.   The diagram
at 167b and c explains the construction of this costume.   To

Fig. 161.   Fig. 162.   Fig. 163.

Fig. 164.   Fig. 165.   Fig. 166.

Fig. 167a.   Fig. 167b.

drape the cloak here shewn (which measures about 45 inches by 60 inches) proceed as follows : Take the corner *b* (Fig. 167*c*) in the left hand, letting the rest of the drapery fall down the back, then pass under the right armpit, across the chest, and throw the corner *a* upwards over the left shoulder ; *a* will hang down at the back, left side. It will be seen that this garment is weighted at the corners, and this weigthing helps to keep it in position.

We may now turn from the Achaemenid style to that of the period shewing Greek influence.

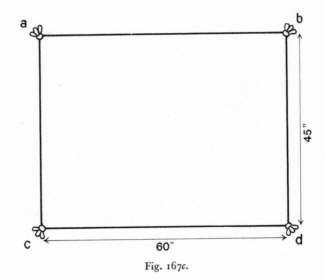

Fig. 167*c*.

Style II

THE STYLE OF THE SELEUCIDS OR SUCCESSORS OF ALEXANDER,
323 B.C.–140 B.C., AND THE ARSACIDS OF PARTHIA,
256 B.C.–A.D. 226.

We do not, in the present state of our knowledge, possess in any considerable numbers examples of Graeco-Persian art. Yet it will be clearly evident that Greek influences prevail in the three examples which follow at Figs. 168, 169 and 170, more especially when the ornamental detail of these costumes is taken into account. In all three there is an unmistakable note which differentiates them from the Achaemenid costumes which precede them and the Sassanid which follow after. Figs. 168 and 169 are from a Parthian (Arsacid) relief on the tomb of King Antiochus I (69 B.C.–34 B.C.), which he built for himself in Northern Asia Minor. The king wears a Persian tiara and over it a crown. His cloak, which is fastened on the right shoulder, may be said to be purely Greek in style. Underneath the cloak there is a long-sleeved tunic, in part tight-fitting but rather full in the skirt and caught up by a band between the legs, a device which would make the garment suitable as a riding-dress. The wreaths of bay or laurel are characteristic of Greek ornament and the powdering of stars upon the tunic is familiar to us from Greek vase-paintings upon which are represented certain Graeco-Asiatic costumes, as, for example, the Phrygian dress.

Fig. 169 is that of the god Mithra-helios (the Persian sun-god). On his head he wears the well-known " Phrygian

Fig. 168   Fig. 169.

Fig. 170.

Bonnet," a common type of male head-dress in the countries bordering the southern coast of the Black Sea and that of Western Asia Minor. It may be described as a soft cap with the top falling towards the forehead, two flaps at either side, which can be fastened, on occasion, under the chin, and a third flap covering the nape of the neck. In the left hand the god carries the Zoroastrian " barsom " or wand of sacred twigs, while in his right he holds the circlet—Persian symbol of sovereignty—with which he is investing the king. For the rest the costume of the god and that of the king are almost identical, and both seem to be wearing the Persian tight-fitting trousers under their long tunics.

Fig. 170 is that of an ancestor of Antiochus from the same source. In this case the main difference between Fig. 170 on the one hand and Figs. 168 and 169 on the other, is that the long coat, tied with ribbons on the breast, which is worn by the ancestor, is purely Persian. Compare with the Achaemenid example at Fig. 158a. The head-dresses of Figs. 169 and 170 are almost identical, and the decoration of both head-dresses and coat is of similar style. As can be seen, the facial type of all three examples is purely Greek and presumably the work of a Greek sculptor.

Style III

SASSANID COSTUME

We now come to the third type of Persian dress, namely, that worn during the Sassanid Dynasty, which dates A.D. 211–A.D. 642. The Greek influence almost disappears with the commencement of this era, and we have a return to the

Persian coat and trousers as far as men's dress is concerned. There is, however, this difference between the tailored suits of the Achaemenids and those of the Sassanids : instead of the plain stiff lines seen in the earlier style, we have garments made apparently of thin silk which is shewn as if fluttering in the breeze. These fluttering draperies are further accentuated by floating ribbons with which the costumes are lavishly garnished, and which are attached not only to the head-dresses, belts and shoes but to almost any point where excuse can be made for their introduction. Then the elaborate head-dress which each Sassanid monarch designed for himself and which distinguishes him from his predecessors, makes the whole style perhaps the most extravagantly fantastic example of men's dress ever known.

Fig. 171 is a representation of an early Sassanid king (Narsē, A.D. 293–A.D. 302). In his dress there is one trace of Greek influence remaining, namely, the cloak, while the rest of his costume is purely Persian. The crown, which seems to be derived from the tiara (Mitra) head-dress, has protruding from the top an immense globe of curled hair which is covered by a veil of gauze. The base of the crown has a band of ribbon tied at the back and shewing wide floating ends. The curling of the long hair is incredibly exaggerated as is also the treatment of the beard and the long ribbons which tie the shoes. The whole costume is evidently made from thin woven material which, as has been said, shews a marked contrast to the Achaemenid stiffness. The boy's costume, Fig. 172, calls for no comment. It is almost identical with that of Fig. 171 except for the hair-dressing which in this case resembles that of Fig. 173, which represents the goddess Anahit who is in the act of investing King Narsē with the royal circlet, here tied with large

fluttering ribbons. The crown of Anahit is surmounted by
a great mound of piled-up curls, but the ringlets of hair which

Fig. 171.   Fig. 172.   Fig. 173.

fall over her shoulders are reminiscent of Greek coiffures—
not those of the Alexandrine era, however, but of the earlier
archaic types which we are familiar with on the vase-paintings

of the sixth and early fifth centuries B.C. There is little to be
said regarding the rest of the costume of this goddess. The
cloak and tunic may be said to shew Greek influence in a
modified form, while the ribbon bows give the Persian
atmosphere. These three costumes, like those of the
remaining Sassanid illustrations, except otherwise stated, are
taken from rock-carvings, which still exist in various parts of
Persia.

Fig. 174 is another Sassanid monarch, Ardashir II,
A.D. 379–A.D. 383. He holds in his hand the royal circlet.
His special head-dress consists of a globe of curls tied by
fluttering ribbons which protrudes from the top of his tall
Persian cap (Kulah) which may, in this case, be made of
precious metal, not of felt, but it has nevertheless the characteristic shape. At the edge of the head-dress there is a
band of ribbon which is tied at the back and has immense
fluttering ends. The hair is worn long and elaborately
curled. A jewelled girdle is wound about the shoulders and
passed under the armpit and lastly it is tied between the
shoulder-blades. We can see in the drawing one end of the
inevitable long fluttering ribbons which finish off this girdle.
The waist-belt is tied in a bow in front and the decoration
of the sword-belt (the " wave-pattern ") is the sole trace of
Greek influence seen in this costume. The tight-fitting tunic
is looped up at each side—a device which would tend to
make it more suitable for riding. Finally, the treatment of
the trousers clearly indicates that they are made from thin
material.

Fig. 175 is a representation of the celebrated Sassanid
monarch, " Barham Gur," A.D. 420–A.D. 438. This drawing
is taken from a silver dish of post-Sassanid work, part of the
collection at the Hermitage Museum (Leningrad). The

13

Fig. 174.

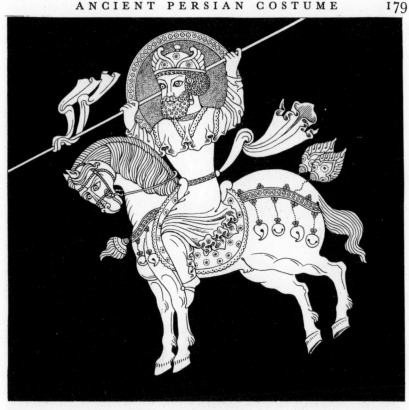

Fig. 175.

king is in hunting-dress.   His tunic, like that of Ardashir II
(Fig. 174), is girded under the arms.   The jewelled belt is
finished at the back by a wide fluttering scarf.   The whole
costume is of pure Persian type and the design of the crown
and treatment of hair and beard seem restrained and simple
when compared, for example, with that of Narsē (Fig. 171).
King Khusraw II, A.D. 590–A.D. 628, is seen at Fig. 176.   It is
from an original now in the Bibliothèque Nationale (Paris).
Like Barham Gur, Khusraw II is in hunting-dress.   His

Fig. 176.

jewelled crown placed low on the brows is surmounted by a
small Persian kulah, also jewelled, as are the eagle's wings,
crescent and globe which are piled up to make this elaborate
and remarkable head-dress.   There is a jewelled girdle
round the shoulders and one round the waist, while in addition we have here a sword-belt and still another belt which
supports a quiver.   This last, by the way, is decorated with
patterns derived from Greek ornament.   The tunic and
trousers worn by Fig. 176 seem to be of thicker stuff than

Fig. 177b.

Fig. 177c.

Fig. 177a.

those of Figs. 171 and 175, and the ornament with which they are covered suggests, somewhat remotely it is true, a Greek source. Fig. 177a represents the goddess Anahit, as she appears when investing Khusraw II with his royal powers. The costume of the goddess does not differ in essentials from that seen at Fig. 173, but at Fig. 177a the jewelled crown is smaller and simpler. It is here surmounted by a pomegranate (a symbol of the goddess) instead of curls of hair. Fluttering ribbons are now much less evident and the cloak seems to be cut on semicircular lines. Fig. 177b is an enlargement of the ornamental detail of the cloak, and Fig. 177c shews one of the arches of the crown on a magnified scale. Fig. 177a to c is taken from a rock-carving, the subject of which is the investiture of Khusraw II. Fig. 178 is from a silver dish in the Hermitage Museum (Leningrad). This is a Sassanid or Parthian bowman. The bow, as will be seen, is of similar shape to that used by Khusraw II (Fig. 176). The tunic seems to be of gauffered material and the high boots with upturned toes suggest a foreign origin. Figs. 179–181 are representations of women's dress of late or post-Sassanid origin. Figs. 179 and 181 are from a silver dish now in the Bibliothèque Nationale (Paris). They are described as " women bearing offerings." These costumes call for little comment ; each wears a double tunic. Fig. 179 has the frequently seen head-veil, but Fig. 181 wears only a bandeau with floating ribbons at the back. Fig. 180, another " woman bearing offerings," is from a Sassanid silver dish in a Russian museum. The long plait of hair and wreath of bay leaves are noteworthy, but the dress differs hardly at all from that of Figs. 179 and 181. On the whole, women's dress during the Sassanid Period seems to have changed little, though the extreme mannerism of the art of this era gives, at first

Fig. 178.

Fig. 179.

Fig. 180.

Fig. 181.

glance, a different effect, in reality the style does not differ greatly from that of Assyrian female costume.

SASSANID ORNAMENT

It will be remembered that the ornament seen on the costumes of the Seleucid and Arsacid Periods was distinctly Greek in character. The same may be said of the Sassanid relief carving at Fig. 182. Practically all the detail here is

Fig. 182.

derived from the Greek, but when the Sassanid textiles are examined we find here a new and distinctive note. Fig. 183, a Sassanid silk pattern, of which both the Victoria and Albert Museum (London) and the Musée des Arts Decoratifs (Paris) possess an example, is woven in a twill and the

Fig. 183.

colouring is of two tones of green.   The linked circles are typical, as is also the heraldic animal which they enclose. There is a remote trace of Greek influence in the ornamental foliage between the circles.   Textile designs of this character became immensely popular in Europe ; not only were they exported from Persia but in succeeding centuries they were actually woven at Constantinople.   One well-known design of Sassanid type is that of the " Elephant pattern " found in the tomb of Charlemagne at Aix-la-Chapelle.   This is said to have been placed in this monarch's tomb when it was opened in the tenth century.   There is a good coloured facsimile of this Elephant pattern in the Victoria and Albert Museum (London).   The Sassanids were overthrown by the Arabs in A.D. 642 ; but Sassanid art did not die.   The conquering dynasty, that of the Abbasids, even adopted the costume of the conquered to some extent.   Thus the romantic and fantastic dress of the Sassanid monarchy has influenced the art of the Islamic Period.   Those legendary Persian monarchs, Jam-shid and Rustam, were not forgotten and we can feel that the whole atmosphere of the *Arabian Nights Entertainment* would not be out of keeping with costumes such as those worn by Barham Gur and Khusraw II.

Finally, we cannot fail to observe the unusual flamboyance of this style when we compare it with those previously illustrated in Egypt and Mesopotamia.   It is possible that the fluttering draperies and ribbons may be partially an artist's mannerism of the period but that cannot be said for the fantastic royal head-dresses as worn by the Sassanid kings. The royal head-dresses of the Egyptian monarchs, namely, the combination of the head-dresses of " the Upper and Lower Lands," while certainly striking, seems quiet and restrained compared with Sassanid variations—while those of the Assyrian kings and those of the earlier Persian monarchs seem steady and dignified in style.   One might say, looking into the future, that it is not until the late Mediaeval and Renaissance periods in Europe we find in men's dress anything so frivolous.

BIBLIOGRAPHY

In the case of those volumes published in the first half of the nineteenth century, consultation is usually only possible in a large reference library ; but, on the other hand, the later authorities are much more accessible.

ANCIENT EGYPTIAN COSTUME

Brunton, W., *Kings and Queens of Ancient Egypt*, 1926.

Carter, H., *The Tomb of Tut-Ankh-Amen*, 1923, 1927 and 1933.
Champollion, J., *Monuments de l'Égypte et de la Nubie*, 1845.

Flinders-Petrie, Sir W., *A History of Egypt*, 1923.

Gardner-Wilkinson, Sir J., *The Manners and Customs of the Ancient Egyptians*, 1840, 1878 and 1890.
Garstang, J., *The Hittite Empire*, 1929.
Gosse, A., *Civilisation in Ancient Egypt*, 1915.

Hall, H., *Ancient History of the Near East*, 1913.
Heuzy, L. and J., *Histoire du Costume dans l'antiquitie classique*, 1935.
Hottenroth, *Le Costume 1883–1892*.

Leemans, C., *Aegyptische Monumenten*, 1839–89.
Lepsius, C., *Denkmaeler aus Ægypten und Æthiopien*, 1849–59.

Maspero, G., *Art in Egypt*, 1921.

Perrol, G. and Chipiez, C., *History of Ancient Egypt* (trans. Armstrong, W.), 1883.
Prisse d'Avennes, E., *Histoire de l'Art Égyptien d'après les Monuments*, 1860.

Racinet, *Le Costume Historique*, 1888.
Ranke, H., *The Art of Ancient Egypt*, 1936.
Rosellini, I., *Monumenti dell'Egitto e della Nubia*, 1832-44.

Wallis-Budge, Sir E., *The Gods of the Egyptians*, 1904.
Weigall, A., *The Glory of the Pharaohs*, 1923.

Catalogues and Publications

British Museum Handbooks and Reproductions.

Cambridge Ancient History, 1923–24.

Encyclopaedia Brittanica, 14th Ed.

Metropolitan Museum of Art, New York, *Picture Book*, 1935.
Metropolitan Museum of Art, New York, Winlock, H., *Treasure of El Lāhūn*, Vol. IV.
Musée du Caire, Vernier, E., *Catalogue Général Antiquités Égyptiennes*, 1927.

ANCIENT MESOPOTAMIAN COSTUME

Botta, M., *Monuments de Ninive*, 1849.

Childe, V., *The Most Ancient East*, 1929.
Conteneau, D., *Civilization d'Assur et de Babylone*, 1937.

Delaporte, L., *Mesopotamia*, 1925.

Gadd, C., *History and Monuments of Ur*, 1929.

Hall, H., *Ancient History of the Near East*, 1913.
Herzfeld, E., *Am Tor von Asien*, 1920.
Heuzey, L., *Costume dans Antiquité L'Orient*, 1935.

King, L., *History of Sumer and Akkad*, 1910.
Koldewey, R., *Excavations at Babylon*, 1914.

Layard, A., *Monuments of Niniveh*, 1849 and 1853.

Olmstead, A., *History of Assyrian Art*, 1923.

Pijoan, J., *History of Art*, 1926.
Place, V., *Ninive et l'Assyrie*, 1867.

Rawlinson, G., *Five Great Monarchies of the Ancient World*, 1871.
Rostoutzeff, M., *A History of the Ancient World* (trans. J. Duff), 1927.

Woolley, Sir L., *The Sumerians*, 1928.
Woolley, Sir L., *Ur of the Chaldees*, 1929.
Woolley, Sir L., *Ur, Excavations, The Royal Cemetery*, 1934.

CATALOGUES AND PUBLICATIONS

Assyrian Sculptures in British Museum, Budge, E., 1914–38.

British Museum, Gadd, C., *The Assyrian Sculptures*, 1934.
British Museum, King, L., *Bronze Reliefs from the Gates of Shalmaneser*, 1915.

Cambridge Ancient History, 1923 and following.

Encyclopaedia Brittanica, 14th Ed.

Musée du Louvre, Conteneau, D., *Catalogue des Antiquités Orièntales*, 1927.
Musée du Louvre, Heuzey, L., *Catalogue des Antiquités Chaldéennes*, 1902.

ANCIENT PERSIAN COSTUME

Dieulafoy, *La Perse, La Chaldée et La Susiane*, 1887.

Flandin, E. and Coste, P., *Voyage en Perse*, 1843 and 1854.

Herzfeld, E., *Archaeological History of Iran*, 1935.
Herzfeld, E., *Iran in the Ancient East*, 1941.
Huart, C., *Ancient Persian and Iranian Civilization*, 1927.

de Morgan, J., *Mission Scientifique en Perse*, 1897.

Perrot, G. and Chipiez, C., *History of Art in Persia*, 1892.
Pope, A., *A Survey of Persian Art*, 1938–39.
Postoutzeff, M., *A History of the Ancient World* (trans. J. Duff), 1927.

PUBLICATIONS

Cambridge Ancient History, 1923 and following.

Encyclopaedia Brittanica, 14th Ed.